DADDY, stop talking!

DADDY, Stop talking!

AND OTHER THINGS MY KIDS WANT BUT WON'T BE GETTING

ADAM CAROLLA

DEY ST.
AN IMPRINT OF
WILLIAM MORROW PUBLISHERS

DEY ST.

HarperCollins books may be purchased for educational, business, or sales promotional use. For information please e-mail the Special Markets Department at SPsales@harpercollins.com.

A hardcover edition of this book was published in 2015 by Dey Street Books, an imprint of William Morrow Publishers.

FIRST DEY STREET BOOKS PAPERBACK EDITION PUBLISHED 2016.

Designed by Paula Russell Szafranski

Title page photograph © by Kwaku Alston.
All other photographs are courtesy of the author.
Illustrations are by Paul Matvienko-Sikar.

Library of Congress Cataloging-in-Publication Data has been applied for.

ISBN 978-0-06-239425-5

16 17 18 19 20   DIX/RRD   10 9 8 7 6 5 4 3 2 1

For my children, Sonny and Natalia.

Thanks for giving me so much material to use in this book.

And to Lynette, for getting me into this mess in the first place.

Despite all my complaints, I love you very much.

❤ ❤ ❤

Contents

DADDY, stop talking!

Introduction: The Culture of Dad Shaming

I'LL GET RIGHT out of the gate with an apology/explanation. I know that, before I had kids, I made a lot of proclamations that I would never become one of those celebrity blowhards who has kids, and then can't stop talking about them and goes and writes a children's book (I'm looking at you Jamie Lee Curtis, Paul McCartney and Madonna) or even worse, a parenting book.

But, as you'll soon read and understand, raising kids is basically a problem you throw money at. Well, I have twins, so I need twice as much money to throw at the problem. Thus, this book. Please don't loan it to your friend. Make them buy their own. In fact if you could plan a Nazi-esque book burning when you're done with this copy so that it can't be passed around, I'd really appreciate it.

This book will be full of tales of the misery that is parenting as a modern male. The days of *Father Knows Best* are long gone. It's no longer enough to be just the breadwinner and disciplinarian. Dads today are expected to be earners, handymen, and spider killers, like we always were—but now all the mommy bloggers have demanded that we're also diaper changers, meal makers and field trip chaperones, too.

Unlike other celebrity parenting books, this one won't be an excuse for me to use my kids to talk about how great a dad and human being I am, with false humility. I can't stand that bullshit when famous folk use their kids as human shields to get windy about how grounded they are. That's just a way of being a blowhard by saying that they're not a blowhard. I can't stand when actors sit down with Billy Bush and say, "When I come home after I leave the set, all I see is a five-year-old who wants to wrestle with Daddy. He doesn't know I'm such a superstar that I've had people taking my picture all day." They're essentially saying, "He doesn't know how great I am!"

I'm also not going to tell you how I learn from my kids. Fuck that. I'm the grown-up. They and, subsequently, you as you read this, are learning from me. I've got no beef with her as an actress, but when Amy Adams won her Golden Globe she did one of those actressy things that drive me insane. She thanked everybody: costars, agents, managers, and so on. Then at the end she thanked her obnoxiously named child, Aviana, a name that I'm pretty sure she took from the sparkling water she was drinking on set. This kid, by her own admission, was not old enough to understand what Mommy was saying. So why did she thank her? Because the little tyke had taught her how to "accept joy and let go of fear." Her daughter was three. She probably only taught Amy how to have a Guatemalan chick take care of her while Mama was on set all day. My twins have taught me basically nothing except that kids are expensive and have no gratitude.

I hate the parent-shaming crap that is so pervasive today. It's like the guy who announces his wife is his best friend. He doesn't mean it; he just does it to make the rest of us look like assholes.

As I write this book, there is an Apple commercial showing how I can be closer with my kids through apps. It shows happy dads connecting with their progeny by using apps to map the stars, garden and take pictures of tidal pools. You know, shit that I never do with my kids because I'm too busy earning the money to buy them the iPhones they use to ignore me. Ads like this are just not realistic. The only thing I do with my phone is watch a little porn, then call my agent and yell at him to find me work so that my kids can enjoy all those app-tivities with the nanny. If this ad were at all realistic, if it looked in any way like my life, it would show the dad screaming at the mother to get the glass replaced on her broken iPhone and then he and the kids staring at their phones while ignoring each other.

I know I've already made the lady readers' uteruses pucker with my insensitivity. Better get used to it. You're only three pages in, there's plenty more to come. Listen, I understand that I'm not the world's greatest dad. You know how I know? Because I was driving behind him the other day. I found myself stuck in traffic recently and noticed an SUV with the "You're Driving Behind the World's Greatest Dad" license plate frame. I immediately got mad at this jerk. I know that he didn't get it for himself. His kids went to the mall, saw that and bought it for him. My problem is that he actually put it on his car. If it were me, this thing wouldn't even leave the garage. It's like the dads wearing those Rainbow Loom bracelets their kids make. Sure, smile when they give it to you, but don't show up for work wearing it the next day. If your daughter brought home an orange freeway cone full of semen, and asked you to wear it like a clown hat, would you? If my kids brought me that license plate frame I'd tell them I was going to keep it in the trunk so it could be closer to my heart. Where are this guy's friends? Why isn't anyone telling him he's an asshole? I know part of my rage is envy. I am jealous that this guy doesn't care what people think of him. But I hate him for shoving his "greatestness" in the face of all of the other dads out there.

Not that I would want to be Father of the Year. Have you ever noticed how when you're named Of the Year for anything it generally comes back to bite you in the ass? The Employee of the Year is always the one who gets caught embezzling and the Teacher of the Year always ends up on the news as a pedophile, so I choose to embrace my mediocrity.

One piece of dad shaming is close to home; in fact it's on my coffee table right now. Underneath my wife's *Self* magazine, which I argue in the narcissistic disaster we call America is a totally unnecessary publication, was a copy of *Parents*. I think we need magazines about how to focus on other people instead of ourselves. I don't know why this was in my house. This is just a device to scare my wife and other rich white folk into not vaccinating their kids and feeling inadequate because they purchased their Christmas ornaments instead of making them by hand. Just like the activities in the Apple ad, no one does the shit this magazine is suggesting. I'm guessing the true purpose of this magazine is just to leave it around so when company comes over they think you're a good parent. How about a magazine called *Earner* with me on the cover?

And I really resent it when people use their kids to try to make me feel guilty. I never use my kids in that "I have to spend time with my family so I can't finish that project" kind of way. I also can't stand people who act like they're the only ones who have kids. You couldn't show up for the job because you had to spend time with your kids? Well, what about me? I have two of them and I'm here waiting on your ass to arrive. I'm not saying that if you have a kid who is gravely ill you should leave him at the hospital to die so that you can help me. But I resent the kid excuse because it makes me feel like I'm the bad dad for compartmentalizing my family life and work life. Would I prefer to be at Disneyland with my kids? Sure, but I have to be on stage earning the bread. By the way, that's a true story. I once returned from a live gig in Detroit to find that the whole family had gone to the Happiest Place on Earth while I was in the Crappiest Place on Earth.

When I was a writer on *Jimmy Kimmel Live*, before I had kids, if there was a weekend shoot planned, the word would get around: "Someone has to go with Uncle Frank to the meatball festival in Conejo." All the writers would say, "Ah, fuck, I don't want to go." Let's be honest, no one wanted to go. But if you had kids you had an automatic out, you were off that list. It would be like, "Hey, man, I have a daughter. I haven't seen her in a week. She has a soccer thing." So the message to all the single dudes? Get in the bus with Uncle Frank. I was actually routinely punished at work for not having kids. And now that I actually have kids, I still don't cash in and use them as an excuse.

By the way, I've been using the word "kid" a lot. This is on purpose, because I find that all these "I'm a better parent than you" assholes tend to use the word "child" instead of "kid." They also like using "home" instead of "house." When parents, especially mothers, get defensive and vocal they tend to say, "When you come into my *home* and use that tone in front of my *child* . . ."

Anyway, before we move on, let me tell you a little bit about my children . . . I mean kids.

My twins were born on June 7, 2006. They were supposed to be pulled from Mama Carolla on June 6, 2006, but even though I'm not superstitious or religious (as if there's a difference) I thought it just seemed weird to have my kids on 666. So we pushed it by a day. I mean, if you had two flight choices, September 11 or September 12, any level-headed person after 2001 would fly on September 12.

Lynette was having a scheduled C-section, so we had the option of delaying it by a day. Actually, on June 5th, Lynette started having contractions and I thought we were going early. I remember that we were watching *The Apprentice* and, like any good husband, I used the TiVo pause button to time the contractions.

The contractions were just those fake Braxton-Hicks things (up until then I thought Braxton-Hicks were the guys who sang "Smoke from a Distant Fire"), and two days later we were in the hospital extracting the kids. At this time, I was doing my morning radio show. Obviously, I couldn't be there, but the show must go on, so Kimmel filled in. I remember sitting in the room listening to my sports guy Dave Dameshek doing his weekly "Jerk Report," instead of listening to the nurses ordering me around and asking to see my wristband every time I came in and out.

Anyway, they were born and were completely healthy. Sonny was six pounds four ounces, Natalia was five pounds twelve ounces. I'm not going to pretend I know which one came out first. That pisses Lynette off. I got the quiz not too long ago. "Which one was born first?" "Um . . . Natalia." "No" "Uh . . . the other one?" "Yes." "And how far apart were they?" "I dunno. Two or three feet?"

Why "Sonny" and "Natalia" you might ask? I'm half Italian and my wife is full-blooded Italian so we wanted Italian-sounding names. Sonny is short for Santino, taken from *The Godfather*. Natalia gets her name from an actress I beat off to . . . I mean interviewed on *Loveline*, Natalia Cigliuti. Ironically, she's from Uruguay and isn't Italian at all but it sounded good, like it was from the old country. When I called Jimmy to reveal the names on the radio show he commented that Sonny and Natalia sounded like an old couple from Brooklyn. "Sonny and Natalia are coming over and they're bringing manicotti." He also pointed out that Sonny's middle name was Richard (Lynette's father's name), which shortens to Dick. So not only did he have a pornish name, "Sonny Dick," but also sounded like my most hated beverage, Sunny D. Then, just for a little extra salt in the wound, Jimmy noted that my kids were born on Prince's birthday. (Though Prince would probably argue he wasn't even born, but created from a purple energy cloud farted by a unicorn.)

I also wanted them to have solid, classic names. Not made up bullshit names we have nowadays. I don't know what's up with all the . . . den names? Aiden, Jayden and Cayden. That's a soap opera name, not a real name. There's no Aiden, Jayden or Cayden who's going to dive on a grenade in Afghanistan to save his platoon. We're all obsessed with giving our kids unique names to make them feel special. A list came out in 2013 and some of the most popular names were Django, Katniss, Atticus, Asher and Serafina. Listen, you're not going to get into Harvard because you have a unique name that a hundred other white parents in your town also thought was unique. Just fucking name your kid Dave and let him go out and carve a life for himself.

A lot of people do the thing when they have twins where they give them both names that begin with the same letter. I was against that from the start. My best buddy growing up, Ray, has three brothers Rob, Ronnie and Rich. I used to always give him *and* his mom shit for this. I mean, how lazy can you be? This came back to bite me in the ass, though. I was once complaining to Jimmy about something stupid Ray had done and the long history of idiotic decisions that family had made. I went on to say that it really said something about how lazy and retarded that whole family was that all the names began with the same letter and that it was probably so that they'd have fewer letters to remember with their already feeble minds. Jimmy then reminded me about his brother Jon, his sister Jill, his mother Joan and his father James. I'll have to remember not to bring that up again in front of his new daughter, Jane.

Speaking of Jimmy, him being my bestie, he was the first to come see the kids when they got home from the hospital. It was kind of awkward, though. He showed up with Sara Silverman, his girlfriend at the time. Lynette was hormonal and feeling overwhelmed with how disorganized things were at home—diaper pail in the wrong place, spider in the bassinet (both true stories, btw), shit like that. So she was crying. I didn't even know they had come in. When they went into the room they just saw Lynette in a heap of tears and me standing there like a stooge. I remember the look from Sara like, "What did you do, you monster?!" This has happened to me more than once. A few years later, Lynette was out of town and I was alone with the kids. Despite being fine most of the night, the minute their nanny walked in, they started crying. She looked at me like I'd been using them as tennis racquets. Another time, Lynette had gone to see the Killers play over at Kimmel's outdoor stage and came home to the kids crying. She sprinted in yelling, "What's going on, what are you doing?" I said, "I was trying to dry her hair in the microwave, what do you think? They're babies, they're crying. But please, feel free to make it my fault."

See, I even get the dad shaming in *my home* about *my children*.

This is a book for you parenting realists out there. Dads who want to crack a beer and go to the garage instead of to Gymboree class, and moms who can't wait to go back to work after maternity leave. This is for anyone who has ever rolled over in bed after a long day of "Mommy Mommy Mommy Daddy Daddy Daddy" and said to your partner, "What the fuck were we thinking?" Don't get me wrong. I love my kids. I just hate what our society has turned parenting into. It used to be enough to feed, shelter and clothe your kid. Now I talk to the dads at the two o'clock Saturday basketball game who just got back from the soccer tournament in San Juan Capistrano that their kid was playing in that same morning. If he skips that hundred-mile round trip, if he blows that off and only goes to the basketball game, he's a pariah. If my dad had put down his cigar and gotten off the sofa, he would have been a saint. So this is a book for all the other dads out there like me, who yearn for the days of a lower bar. You're welcome.

CHAPTER 1

☞ Daddy, Stop Talking!

SOMETIME SHORTLY AFTER the twins started talking, they decided I should shut up. It quickly became the family joke to teach them to tell Daddy to zip it. I remember one night we were sitting around watching television as a family and I was pausing the TiVo and yapping, as I'm prone to do. Natalia, whom I'm sure had been coached by Lynette, chimed in with "Quiet time, Daddy." This delighted Lynette and also the nanny, Olga, who was sitting with us. Before Natalia could even talk she'd been trained by Lynette to flap her hand open and closed like a duck bill and say "Pa-peep, Pa-peep, Pa-peep," the Italian variation on "You're talking too much." Once it got a laugh, she kept going with it. Eventually the phrase became "Daddy, stop talking." I was on stage doing a charity auction once at the Feast of San Gennaro and the kids were on stage with me. Natalia grabbed the mic and started saying, "Daddy, stop talking." I shot back, "If Daddy stops talking, you don't get a pony."

That's what this book is about. This isn't just a book, it's an act of defiance. Everyone in my life is trying to shut me up. But when I shut up, so does my wallet. This is how Daddy pays for all the events you drag him to that annoy him, that house full of your crap and all the concerts, restaurants and camps you go to while Daddy is out hustling.

It isn't just Natalia. One weekend in 2012, Lynette was out of town (again. See a pattern here?) and I was taking care of the kids. But we called her to check in and say good night. She asked Sonny how things were going with Daddy and he told her, "He's wasting my time." Apparently, Sonny had very important Play-Doh to get to or something because he felt I was talking a little too much. I brought him onto the podcast a day or two later to break it down. He said, "You were talking to me until dinner time," and, infamously, "It's just a waste of my time." This sound clip, a "drop" as we call them in the radio game, became so popular that we turned it into

a ringtone and sold about eight thousand dollars' worth of them. Since then, Sonny has been pestering me for his cut. Literally. Like everyone else in my life, the kids want all of my money. Recently, I had Sonny on stage with me for a corporate event and he started hitting me up for his end of the ringtone money again. I said, "You're living in it, you little shit."

Another time, I was sitting down for dinner with the kids in a diner. Natalia had a grilled cheese and Sonny got a ham sandwich and French fries. At a certain point, I reached over and took a bite of Sonny's sandwich. (Carbs don't count if they're on someone else's plate.) I knew he wasn't going to finish it, and I'm not into wasting food, especially food I pay for. He looked up at me and said, "You have a huge mouth in two ways. You take huge bites of stuff *and* you never stop talking."

My initials are ALC (Adam Lakers Carolla) but they might as well be ATM. My kids experience, but don't appreciate, the nonstop stream of money and stuff in their lives. There is zero connection for them between what Daddy does and the things they enjoy.

One night, I was going between jobs. I had done *The Soup* that night, and had to go straight to the studio to record the podcast. This was around eight, so I called the kids while I was driving to touch base and tell them I loved them. I told Lynette to put Natalia on. She said, "Hi, Daddy," and, before I could start to do the good night, I love you speech she started putting in a gift order. She wanted a Rapunzel doll. I told her I was just calling to say good night. She followed up, "But you're working, right?" She was so used to me calling her from the road, which meant I would be bringing back some crap from the airport gift shop. I explained I was still in town, and I had just had a busy day and didn't have a chance to come home. She kept going. I had to stop her, "You're not getting anything, I'm here." When the phone got handed to her it was like she pulled up to the speaker at the Jack In The Box drive-through. She just started firing her order at me.

I think everything I'm talking about here—the zero appreciation from our kids—can be summed up in the story of a New Year's Eve gig in Reno. The New Year's Eve of 2011 going into 2012, I had a stand-up show in Nevada two nights in a row.

Since I was going to be working over New Year's I decided to make it a family trip. Instead of staying at the Nugget, where I was playing, we'd get a suite in an upscale hotel in Tahoe and have a little family time during the day. I used the American Express Platinum Card, so we got stepped up to an even bigger room, one hundred dollars in WAM (that's Walking Around Money) and we had comps to the buffet. And because it was New Year's Eve they were pouring glasses of Champagne at the counter. After we checked in and got to the room Lynette said, "You know, I'd like some of that Champagne." I asked, "Why didn't you get some?" She brushed it off. Then, a moment later, she said she wanted to go to the store and grab some crackers and junk for the kids, and some Champagne. I told her to grab me some, too. I settled in to watch a little *SportsCenter* before it was time for me to head out to Sparks to do my show while she hit the store. A little while later, she came back with the kids and the cookies and a mini-bottle of Veuve Clicquot.

I asked her, "Where'd you get that?" She said, "I got it at the store." I shot back, "You didn't want to go to the counter and get the freebies?" She replied, "I was at the store." Against my better instincts, I followed up, "But you paid for it with the hundred-dollar credit from the hotel, right?" Of course, her answer was no. Then, to make matters worse, I asked, "Where was the store?" She said, "Right next to the front desk." So she got a thirty-three-dollar mini-bottle of champagne containing three glasses' worth when she could have gotten two for free, mere feet from where she spent my money instead of the WAM from the hotel.

Whatever. I tried to move on as she poured each of us a glass. Then she sat in a chair to leaf through a magazine and put the glass on the floor. I suggested that probably was not a great plan with two kids walking around. As predicted, three sips in, the glass was knocked over by Sonny. As I watched eleven dollars soaking into the padding of the carpet, I downed my glass, then said I was going to take a nap.

I woke up about half an hour later and said, "Let's go out to dinner before I have to head to Reno." We wrangled the kids and, as we were walking out, I saw a full glass sitting on the table. Again, the mini-bottle could only contain three glasses. One was in my belly, one was in the carpet, so this was a third one poured by Lynette for herself. I asked, "What's up? Are you gonna drink that?" She said yeah and began walking toward the door. I stopped her. "No, drink it now," I said. Confused, she asked, "What?" I said, "Drink it." So she took a sip. Not good enough. I said, "No, finish it. We're not wasting that." I made her drink the whole goddamn thing.

Cut to the following morning and time for breakfast. They all want room service. This is a nice hotel with a very nice buffet upstairs that, again, is *free*. So I say no, we have a free buffet, let's go check it out. I win that battle and we head upstairs to the buffet, which is a horn of plenty: five different kinds of sticky buns, omelet bar, fresh fruit and so on. Of course, in the face of all this food, there is only one move for Natalia. She scans the entire buffet like the Terminator analyzing the room looking for his target. She's trying to find the one item they don't have. She does so, and announces that she wants chocolate-chip pancakes. I told her, "You can have eggs any way you want, waffles, sweet rolls . . ." No dice. She wanted chocolate-chip pancakes and that was that. And Lynette backed her play. She found a way to make me pay.

It's not the money. That was eight bucks or something. It's the principle. We have this whole spread in front of us that, again, is free and they still want more. There was a Mexican guy in a hat who would make you any kind of omelet you want. Nope. She needed the one thing they didn't have. There were Belgian waffles, toast, sticky buns, biscuits—every combination of flour, eggs, sugar and butter imaginable, except pancakes. Come to think of it, there might have been pancakes but no chocolate chips. Thus, she needed the chocolate-chip pancakes.

The next day, Natalia wanted chocolate-chip pancakes again. I put my foot down. I wanted to send a message. The terrorists hate us because of what was in that buffet. There were two hundred and thirty-three food options. I wasn't going to let something that would have been the greatest day of my childhood be so wildly unappreciated. I told her to go find something and eat. She walked in, grabbed a sticky bun and a little melon and was fine. But I got a heaping helping of the stink eye from Lynette.

The whole trip, and my whole point, really came into focus when we were going home. After leaving Tahoe and heading towards the airport in Reno to fly back, we passed a big billboard with my picture advertising the shows. I said "Hey, kids, look. See your old man up there?" They were completely unfazed. It might as well have been a billboard for a local RV dealership. I banged a U-turn and went back for a second lap to see if I could muster a modicum of enthusiasm from the kids. But like so many who have gone to Reno before, I came up snake eyes.

That story might make you think I'm a horrible dad and a greedy asshole ogre. But by the end of this book I also hope to lay out a strong defense for why being a dad in today's society will drive me insane and possibly to an early grave.

I am reminded of a conversation I once had with Mark McGrath of Sugar Ray. Mark is a great guy and genuinely funny. One Sunday afternoon we were sitting around at Kimmel's watching football and

shooting the shit. In that conversation I asked him where Sugar Ray was playing and he joked about their fall from stardom and that they were now playing "anywhere you can smell funnel cake." Nothing beats a nice *and* humble guy. But the thing he said that sums up perfectly how I feel about my current lot in life as a father and husband is this. Mark is also a father of twins and stated perfectly the thing that is constantly on my mind: "Since when did making all the money count for nothing?"

He's right. Keeping the lights on, paying the mortgage, feeding the kids, going out and earning all day at whatever profession you have is now a zero. That gets you back to even. This is not an indictment of our families; it's just how our culture has gone. It's like smoking pot. Back in the 1950s it was considered an activity second only to bestiality in how deplorable it was. Now everyone is firing up everywhere, no problem. You can't go to the Mac store without getting a contact high. What would have been unimaginable and shameful back in the day is common and accepted.

Divorce lawyers, start your engines. If any part of this book is going to lead to the end of my marriage, it's what I'm going to say next. But it has to be said: women are no longer holding up their part of the societal bargain. Men were supposed to bring home the bacon and women were supposed to cook it. That just isn't the case these days.

One morning, I walked in to see Lynette watching a rerun of *I Love Lucy*. It was an episode in which Ricky was complaining to Lucy about how hard it was being a working man, and Lucy returning the complaint that it is very hard cooking, cleaning and keeping up a house. Then it went into the hackneyed sitcom premise of them switching roles. I feel like that lame-ass idea was part of every sitcom produced before 1990. Lucy had to get out the help-wanted ads and find a job, which she inevitably failed at, but Ricky also learned a valuable lesson by fucking up the eggs and toast that he had to make for his breadwinner wife.

So I'm watching Lynette watch this show about gender roles after having made my own coffee and breakfast, which consisted of dumping some Planters peanuts into a cup. I realized that this premise would never fly today. Men have work-work and housework. It's demeaning for women to cook and clean. But if a man decided he wasn't going to go out and earn a living, he'd be considered a deadbeat. My house has a maid, and my kids have a nanny that I pay for. If my wife was the one out working, and I was the one getting mani-pedis and sushi while the maid cleaned and the nanny took the kids to soccer practice, all her friends would say, "Why are you still with that moocher?"

Not an exaggeration, by the way. I came home from a gig at the Wiltern Theater in Los Angeles, probably the biggest venue I've ever played, to find green and blue nail polish on Sonny's fingers and toes. The androgyny part aside, the thing that really pissed me off was that Lynette had taken herself and the kids for mani-pedis, while I was sweating my ass off onstage with Jay Mohr in front of 1,850 people.

Nowadays, telling your wife "I have to work" gets you a disappointed sigh. This is the worst period in history to be a dad. It used to be that if you worked and provided that was enough. On the weekend, you tossed the ball around with your boy or had a tea party with your little girl, and that was plenty. Now we're expected to be present for every kindergarten graduation and bowel movement our kid makes, applauding them the entire time, while simultaneously keeping the bank account full. And all the loser dads who have trust funds or wives who bring home all the money make earners like me look like shit.

So I don't agree with the assertion that I'm an asshole misogynist because I think it would be nice to smell a little pot roast when I come home. Going through a ten-hour day, and then coming home to flip a coin to see who's going to head down the hill and pick up the Chinese food that then eliminates the money earned in the last hour of that ten-hour day just sucks.

I suspect that this is because the workplace has changed. At the turn of the last century, guys used to go to work in a hole in the ground or out on a farm or in a factory. They'd come home covered in coal dust, except for the salt outline from their sweat stains. That was if they even came home at all. Work was more dangerous back then, and thus was appreciated. So when their ass hit that wooden chair at the dinner table at the end of the day, there was some fucking lasagna waiting.

My problem is that coming home with makeup on and complaining about the satellite delay to *The O'Reilly Factor* doesn't garner me much sympathy. I nearly killed myself doing construction before show business, but the fact is that I'm killing myself now, too. It sucks sometimes, and I need my family to know this.

An example of the disconnect between my kids' lifestyle and how I provide it for them came this year when I was filming my show, *Catch a Contractor.* For those who haven't seen the series, the premise is that I go to houses that have been destroyed by shoddy/shady/shitty contractors who show up just long enough to get the people's money and then leave them in a death trap. Me and my co-host, a talented licensed contractor, Skip, lure the contractor into a sting house, present him with the evidence of his hack work and make him fix it under our supervision. It's a good premise and unlike many of my prior TV projects is executed very well. But it's also filmed in the middle of fucking nowhere. The commutes to and from these dumps are many, many hours in Southern California traffic. I then have the pleasure of confronting sociopaths and comforting destroyed families. It's a real drain. I literally had to break up a fight between two ex-Marines, one being a contractor who screwed over an old service buddy, leaving him with fire-hazard wiring and his ten-month-old daughter crawling around on asbestos-covered floors.

The one that took the cake was in Watts. That's the section of South Central Los Angeles that was destroyed by riots in 1965, and looks like it still hasn't recovered. This is not a place you want to be. And the place you least want to be in Watts is crammed in a poorly renovated six-by-eight windowless bathroom with two cameramen, blazing hot lights, stuck between an angry Mexican contractor and an even angrier black homeowner. I'm standing there yelling at a contractor, "Look at this open sewage pipe, these people have been breathing this," and then realizing I'm breathing it in myself.

The only thing that could make my day worse was knowing

where my kids were at that moment. The night before, I checked my schedule, and saw that it was time for the Watts bathroom shoot. I was complaining to Lynette about having to go back there and asked her what her plan was for the day. She told me it was Presidents' Day so the kids were off school. That meant big plans. "Natalia, her friend Cami, Cami's mom, Sonny and I are taking a helicopter to Catalina to go zip-lining." You literally couldn't be doing something more opposite from what I was doing. Zip-lining in the open air on a Pacific island, versus a bathroom in Watts as spacious as an MRI tube.

I guess I must have been so busy I missed the Evite. I don't begrudge them enjoying their time; I just want acknowledgment for my part in making it possible for them. I've always said when people ask me about career goals that I would like to be successful enough to enjoy the life my wife and kids have.

So my kids will eventually get their wish and Daddy will stop talking, due to the massive coronary I suffer from busting ass to provide for them. With that in mind I'd like to use this book to also lay down some fatherly wisdom they'll need when hitting those big life events—specifically buying your first car, buying your first house, and hitting puberty—since I won't be around to dispense it. Think of it as mediocre parenting from beyond the grave. The sections specifically for Sonny and Natalia to read at those milestones will be marked with this graphic.

And you, dear reader, may also see these graphics.

This is to let not just Sonny and Natalia, but all of you, know to strap in and prepare to get hit with some serious pearls and nuggets of truth. The Aceman is about to say something heavy and lay down a great concept that you need to dig.

And . . .

This is to signify my ideas: all the apps, gadgets, products and systems that I've come up with to make parenting, or just life in general, better.

I hope that all you readers dig these concepts and inventions because again I'm sure when it comes to Sonny and Natalia all of this wisdom will fall on four deaf ears. I tried to drop some knowledge on Natalia not so long ago and she shot back, "I don't have to listen to you. I'm not one of your assistants."

CHAPTER 2

☞ Your Home Is Not Your Castle

THE HOUSE THAT the kids were first brought back to from the hospital was a 1929 Spanish-style home. It was more than a fixer-upper. I did a meticulous, total nut-and-bolt restoration of that place. I painstakingly turned it into a centerfold for *Architectural Digest*. It was a museum to my cars and monument to my craftsmanship. It even had a name: Vista del Lago. When your house has a name, you know you've arrived. But when the twins came along, all that shit went out the window. When you have children the idea that a man's home is his castle no longer applies. Your home just becomes a place to store their crap.

When you have kids, your castle becomes their bouncy castle. In my case, this is literally true. Jimmy Kimmel bought Sonny and Natalia this inflatable castle in 2012. It's the real deal. At first, I thought he had rented it. No, he bought it.

It's nice having rich friends who can blow a bunch of money on great gifts for your kids, but it really makes you look like a loser. I'm positive that my kids are secretly planning a Menendez-style killing so that they can live with their rich Uncle Jimmy and get lavished with bouncy castles and audioanimatronic ponies (an actual Kimmel Christmas gift in '08).

I didn't have the space for the bouncy castle, and, in order to simultaneously go for the World's Coolest and World's Worst Dad title, I moored it to the pool. Before you call child protective services, the fan was off to the side, so they wouldn't get electrocuted. I'm not a monster.

Technically, you can't have an orgasm at age six, but when he saw this setup, Sonny was close. They were sliding down that thing for weeks. This kind of luxury would have been unimaginable for a young Adam Carolla. It is not just that my parents were cheap. These kinds of things didn't even exist back then. Why not? Did we not have fans and burlap in the 1970s? Sonny has spent more time in bouncy houses than I did in my regular house when I was his age. I was out on the streets trying to get away from my family as much as possible. He's so used to being in bouncy castles that I wouldn't be surprised if he showed up at his first job interview not wearing shoes and complaining that the carpet didn't have enough spring to it. It's going to be an issue later in life, I'm convinced. Sonny is going to off himself at twenty because his pleasure center will be burned out like someone who did too much coke in the 1970s.

This thing literally covered my pool for a month, but at least I knew where it was. Usually, I find my kids' crap by stepping on it in the middle of the night.

Ugh. Legos. I'm happy Sonny is into building stuff, but if I step on one more fucking Lego I'm gonna go loco. I remember thinking when I was a kid that Legos would never last. Who knew they'd be the biggest thing ever and that every movie would also have a Lego version that my kids would need to buy the toy version of? It's a great scam. *Iron Man* comes out and you need to take the kids to see it and get the Iron Man figure. Then Lego does an animated "Lego Iron Man" DVD and you have to buy that *and* the Lego set that goes with it. I should come out with a Lego version of this book and make some extra cash.

Sonny is into the Ninjago Legos, which are particularly awful to step on in the middle of the night. As if the eight corners of your standard Lego block weren't enough to puncture your heel, these fuckers are carrying spears and throwing stars. I was walking down the hall one night carrying a glass of red wine, and one of these Ninjago spears went into my bare foot and I ended up dumping the whole glass of wine on the carpet.

Not only did I think Legos would go the way of dodos, I can't believe how long ninjas have hung on. Once the gun was invented, shouldn't our fascination with the ninja have ended? Yes, you have a black belt. But is that belt thick enough to stop this bullet, bitch? Sonny is crazy for ninjas. I don't know why. I think it's a waste of time. What are the chances he's going to grow up to become a ninja? Seriously, how many kids are going to parlay that fascination into a thriving career in ninja-ing? I'm going to show him a picture of Larry Flynt and tell him "this guy could take out ten ninjas if he had a gun on his lap so quit giving them so much credit."

If it's not Ninjago spears piercing the soles of my feet, it's a fake spider or rattlesnake freaking me out when I stumble around half-drunk in the middle of the night. What happened to robots and rocket ships? I'm not going to head downstairs for my third tumbler of Mangria and think a miniature robot broke into the house. But if I see the fake rattlesnake in the dark through my boozy filter, I'm going to attack it with a mop handle.

Sonny's Legos did provide a cute moment one day, though. He had a new Lego set, and the box said "Ages 5–8." So he came up to me and asked, "Dad, are you the right age to help me put this together?" I laughed. It was really cute how he thought that once you were past eight you couldn't build with Legos anymore. Of course, I told him I was too old and went to take a nap.

So finding the kids' stuff is very easy when they lose it. Just take off your shoes and walk around in the dark, and you'll find every Ninjago spear and fake tarantula you've ever paid for. But you know what I can't find? My shit.

As a parent, you can fill your house with toys, as I have, and the kids will still go for every item you want them to leave alone. Their favorite toy when they were two was my alarm clock. They were constantly messing with it. They'd take it down, pull the plug, remove the batteries, take a leak on it and beat it with bats like Joe Pesci and his brother at the end of *Casino*. My house looked like a Gymboree, but they were still attracted to the only thing that I needed them to not screw with. It was either the alarm clock or the universal remote. (Which I still think should come with a button that you hold for four seconds to put in lock mode. That way kids can't go monkeying with it.) The twins' hit list of shit to mess with when they were terribly two was: #1 my alarm clock, #2 my universal remote, #3 the wrapper from my wife's protein bars, #4–#9 anything I didn't want them to play with and #10 their toys.

The worst is when in addition to playing with your stuff, they hide it. A few years back, Lynette lost her iPhone. The kids must have been five or six at the time. We searched high and low for a week, and couldn't find it anywhere. Eventually, we gave in and spent the four hundred bucks to replace it. Of course, twenty-four hours after we spent that four hundred bucks it magically turned up. Natalia brought it down from the upstairs bathroom, saying that she found it underneath the rug.

Now, mind you, this is the shared bathroom at my previous abode, which had double doors and the Jack and Jill sinks. (By the way, I put the jack in that Jack and Jill bathroom.) This was the family bathroom, the one everyone brushed their teeth in, the one that the kids took baths in. It got the most traffic. Natalia claimed that after a week of looking for and not finding the iPhone, she simply stumbled across it sticking out from underneath the corner of the three-by-two bathmat. There is absolutely no way that with everyone in and out brushing their teeth and bathing not one of us spotted it. I think there was foul play involved. Natalia did get a twenty-dollar finder's fee.

When something gets lost, I want to either never find it again or, at a minimum, find it a week later, twenty-eight miles away washed up on a beach. The part where you find it in your own home a day after you pay to replace it is a cosmic fuck you, on top of the underhanded behavior of your children.

I'm Sick of My Kids Being Sick

Plus kids are always sick and that means a mess. If it's not piles of snotty tissues, it's puke. I'm not sure why, but my son was yakking all over the house the other day and the cleanup job was going to be massive. You know it's bad when you skip right over paper towels and go for something to scoop it up instead. On those days, you end up creating a makeshift excavator out of the *Pennysaver* and a flip-flop.

Vomit is the worst thing you can ever clean up. There's snot rockets, wizz and loogies, but puke is the worst thing the human body can produce to remove from a rug. But the people who do the vomiting, especially when they're children, don't have to clean it up. When they're kids, they're sick and just collapse back into bed and moan while Mommy and Daddy bust out the Lysol wipes. When they're adults, they're passed out in the back of your car while you head to the gas station to put a quarter in the vacuum. If you vomit at school, the janitor has to throw down that sawdust and scoop it up. Even if you vomit in a restaurant because you ate too much, some poor Mexican has to mop it up. I vomited in an icemaker in Tijuana and I sure as shit didn't clean that up. But if you knock over a cup of coffee, *you* clean it up. Why not the vile substance that you actually produce?

I'd like to watch a never-ending reel of people trying to get adults who vomited to clean it up themselves. Forcing drunks to sop up their own sick while their head is still throbbing and they can't stand would be a viral video sensation, I'm convinced.

Vomit really tells you where you stand in life. There is a sweet spot when it comes to vomiting or seeing someone vomit. You don't want people constantly puking around you, but if you haven't seen someone vomit in the last twelve years, you probably aren't experiencing life to the fullest. The optimal position is not having yakked in a long time yourself, but having seen a buddy puking into a trash can at a ball game or a concert in the past five months. I'm proud to say that I haven't upchucked in several years. I have a good constitution, and I'm a heavyweight when it comes to drinking.

Plus, I hate it so much. Even worse than the vomiting itself is that moment when you think you're done puking and the nausea creeps up again. You know, that moment when you've been puking all night, you've burst the blood vessels in your eyes and you've been laying on the filthy tile floor of a frat-house bathroom and you feel like you've finally evacuated everything . . . and then that queasy feeling comes back again.

There are too many question marks about hell to really be scared of it: how hot is it really going to be, who's going to be there and so on. Because, when you think about it, there's probably going to be a lot of cool dudes and whores in hell. It might be a good time. But the nausea that breaks the blissfully ignorant feeling that the vomit storm has passed, that queasy moment when you know the yack is back, if you told me that was hell I would straighten up and fly right for the rest of my life. I'd be the second coming of Mother Teresa.

Anyway, the cleanup. Sonny, you're on notice. Next vomit, you're cleaning up. Then later when you're older and Dad is drunker, I'm going to puke and guess who's cleaning it up? Get the dustpan, boy, and don't go asking the maid for help. Speaking of . . .

Maids and Nannies

Hillary Clinton wrote that book saying that it takes a village to raise a child. She was right. That village was in Guatemala, but now it's in my house. (By the way, my next book will be about gay parents and called *It Takes the Village People*.)

We had hired help from day one. We had to. When Sonny and Natalia were born, I was working my morning radio show while shooting my first independent movie, *The Hammer*, at the same time. So I would have to get up at four forty-five, roll into the studio, do four hours of unscripted comedy and interviews, then head out for several more hours of shooting (and essentially directing) an indie movie. With that schedule, there was no way I was going to physically be able to get up at three, feed and burp the kids and go back to bed. So the first thing we did was hire a night nurse. Again, throw money at the problem. When my kids were first born, I was just going around with a T-shirt cannon stuffed with twenties, firing it at people to get them to change, burp and nurse the kids while I went out and earned said money.

And who cares. The kids didn't know at the time and it's not like they're going to sit me down when they're older and say, "How come you didn't have the guts to sit in my room when I was three weeks old and watch me shit myself?"

Let me start with a fuck you to all the people who are reading this and thinking, "Quit complaining about how hard raising kids is, rich guy. You've got a nanny and a maid." Yes. But I didn't wait in some magical line and get them assigned to me by the government. I pay for them.

And I pay them well. Here's a great rich-guy move that says something about who I am. Two years ago, I heard my kids saying goodbye to Olga for the day, shouting, "Happy Birthday, Olga!" (When they were first learning to talk, they couldn't say her name correctly, so the mispronunciation just stuck.) I didn't know that it was Olga's birthday, so I asked Lynette what we got her. She told me Olga had been having issues with her car, and that we paid three hundred dollars to get it fixed. So I grabbed Olga before she left and asked her what was wrong with the car, what the year and model was—all those dude questions. I was impressed that she knew the mileage. Most people, and sadly most straight guys today, couldn't tell you the mileage on their car. It was a 2002 Camry with 123,000 miles on it. I asked her how much it cost, and she said she didn't know. I was curious how she could remember the mileage, but not how much she paid for it. She said, "You bought it for me."

I had no recollection of buying her a car. Apparently in '06 when the kids were born, I purchased her said '02 Camry to drive them around in. After this revelation, I asked Dr. Drew what it said about me that I had zero recall of buying her a car and the hugs and thanks she swore she gave me at the time. He thinks my lack of self-esteem doesn't allow me to register things that feel good. That's probably pretty accurate, because I'm now about to list all the things that piss me off about having maids and nannies running around my house, instead of all the good things they do for me and my family.

Don't get me wrong. I love Olga. I love what she's doing for my kids. I have almost no complaints. She's helping them learn Spanish, which will be very handy in Los Angeles—which by the time they're in high school will be referred to as North Tijuana. But one issue I do have with Olga is how she calls Natalia "Mama." I know this is a Latino thing, but I don't like it. I don't understand the deal with calling eight-year-olds "Mama." It's always the kids and the elderly that get this name. They don't call anyone "Mama" who can actually be a mother. The ones who haven't sprouted their first pube, and the ones whose eggs are powdered are "Mamas," but the actual mamas not so much. I know that this can't be helping the teen pregnancy rate in the Latin community. When you start calling a kid "Mama" at age four, you're pretty much prepping them to become actual mamas by age twelve.

The second issue I have is what I have termed the Nan-boree. Every couple of weeks, I'll come home to find that my driveway is full and my house is a swarm of wealthy white kids all brought over by Olga's underground nanny network. They have big nanny parties where they get all the kids together and essentially let them roam free while they drink my coffee and chat. I'm fine with that, it's just that it always seems to happen during the very rare opportunities I have to be home in between gigs trying to grab a nap or do some work from home, like calling into radio shows to promote the podcast or writing books like this one.

Interruption is a constant theme in my house, and it is not just caused by my kids. I had a run-in with our maid just the other day. It was eight-thirty in the morning, and I was sitting at the computer in my bathrobe, letting gas pass with my first cup of coffee, as I do loud and proud when I'm in my own home. Then she did the simultaneous knock and enter.

What is that all about? What does that accomplish? The point of knocking is to warn the person who's farting or beating off that you're about to catch them in the act. If you do the simultaneous knock and enter, you don't give them enough time to holster their junk, only enough time to look horrified as you catch them dick in hand. You're supposed to knock and wait for a response or just barge in, but not both. Now I have the humiliation of you catching me in the act *and* the horrible moment right before that, when I know it's going to happen. If you're going to shoot me, just put a bullet in me while I sleep. Don't wake me up and let me see the gun in my face first.

So a couple of hours later, my maid was cleaning the bathroom and I innocently turned the corner. She then did what I believe to be the greatest contribution by Latin women to our nation . . . the screaming of "AIIIEEE!" It was startling. It sounded like she got her tit caught in the slide mechanism of the drawer she was cleaning. How frightened can you possibly be? It's my house and you saw me earlier. I'd understand if you saw me pop up behind you in *your* bathroom on a Sunday, but once you're in *my* house don't be surprised when you see me. What am I supposed to do, phone you ten minutes before and tell you that I'm going to be entering my kitchen? Her scared reaction then got me scared. I ended up being more startled by her reaction than she was by my entering the room. It was a chain reaction of unnecessary fear.

As a side note, Hispanic women, you shouldn't be as jumpy as you are. You come from a land where finding a duffel bag full of heads is a common occurrence. Why do you leap out of your skin when I step into my own kitchen to top off my coffee?

Then Olga got me a few weeks later. This time I was on the shitter. You're supposed to knock and then wait for a response like "Excuse you!" "Wait a second" or "My anus is dilated" (okay, maybe that last one is a little wordy and personal). Again, there was no pause between the knock and her entering the room. Of course she found me on the shitter, because there was nothing I could do in the three-tenths of a second she gave me to react. So why bother knocking at all? Why not just kick the door in and do a shoulder roll like a SWAT team if you have no intention of actually pausing long enough to hear if a noise comes from the other side of the door?

And to you assholes who feel the need to point out that I could lock my bathroom door: One should not have to lock one's bathroom door while in one's home making a number two.

So Long, Sex Life

While we're on locks, let's discuss the well-known but tragic fact that having kids also means that your sex life is pretty much over. This is why there's so much fucking in hotels. When parents actually do manage to get away from the kids for a weekend, that hotel room becomes Sodom and Gomorrah because there have been so many thwarted boning opportunities at home.

I've always recommended getting a barrel bolt on the bedroom door, so if Mommy and Daddy are humping, the kids can't just bust in and ruin it. Unless you're a perv and are into that.

As a builder, I can tell you that there are three kinds of knobs: the dummy knob that you have on the hall closet door or the pantry, it's only on one side and doesn't turn. Then there's the passage knob, which does turn and has two sides, but doesn't lock. This is the kind you have on your bedroom closet or den. Then there's the privacy knob. This locks on the back side so people can't just stroll into the room. It's not going to stop a gangbanger who's throwing a shoulder into it, but will ensure the kids don't walk in, traumatize themselves and ruin one of your infrequent hump-ortunities.

The kiddie interruption thing has happened to us. Lynette and I have been going at it when the kids started banging on the door while we were banging on the bed. When I shout, "Come back in a minute!" Sonny usually walks away, but Natalia keeps knocking and giving her list of demands. I think she's more aware of Mommy and Daddy's special time. Once, when she was just a little under five, I told her to go play because Mommy and Daddy needed some "private time." She replied, "Mommy's gonna look at Daddy's privates?" I thought, "Damn, she figured it out."

At the same time, I've got to admit as a guy you can use this to your advantage. If you know the kids are home and awake you can tell the wife, "Hey, we just have time for a quickie. I mean, usually I'm Sting with the hours-long tantric sex. There's some sitar, a lot of oral. But the kids are in the other room watching *Dora,* so I'm not going to take my shoes off and I'll just put my TV dinner on your back. Cool?"

 I've tinkered with the idea of an app that creates the sound of a child knocking on the door so guys can go into hyper-drive and just finish up quick. Just set it on the nightstand before hitting the sheets and set the countdown clock.

Of course, when it comes to sex, there is a big difference between men and women. Women care about circumstance and atmosphere. Men don't. We're mechanical. There are sex dolls for guys. There's no version of that for women. Women need to be in the mood. The wife can't get into it when she can hear the kids downstairs. For guys, having the kids downstairs watching *Barney* just lets us know that it's game on. That's a half hour we know we're able to bang.

Having kids has messed with the most intimate relationship I have, with my own hand. Not in quantity, but in quality. I always thought that when I got married and had kids I would cut back on the beating off. I assumed having a wife to have sex with and kids running around, especially a daughter, would throw a wet blanket on the whole activity. Not so. In fact, I've probably doubled down on the jacking off.

As I said, my house is a beehive of activity with nannies chasing kids, gardeners blowing leaves and maids running vacuums. But every once in a while I find myself alone and have the following conversation: "Hey, dick?" "Yeah, Adam?" "You ready to party?" "Let me check with the balls. But they're like lunchmeat, they're always ready." I should rename my dick Andy Dick, because it's always down to party.

So I'm alone with a magical box containing two hundred and thirty-five thousand hours of pornography from across the globe and throughout time. I could spend the rest of my life looking at it, and believe me I'm trying, and still not see it all. It's a wonderwall of debauchery—anal, interracial, vintage, German-stump porn— whatever you're into, it's there for you.

Sorry, fellas, for outing us, but ladies, if you ever get this call on your cell phone, you know your guy is ready to have at himself. "Hey, honey, just checking in. Where are you?" We usually don't give a shit. But now we want the GPS coordinates and approximate travel speed. We're triangulating your position to maximize beat-off time. "At the mall? Huh. Nearby mall or the faraway mall? Just curious. Just curious . . . oh, you just got there? Good. Take your time. Relax. Try out that massaging chair at the Brookstone. You deserve it. Don't rush home. But when you do leave, just give me a call . . . so I know you're safe. In fact, just let it ring once and then hang up. And then as you're pulling up the driveway just give a toot-toot on the horn so I know you're home." We actually want to know when you're pulling in the driveway so we can finish pulling on our penis and pull up our pants.

So alone with the porn-u-copia, you start having at yourself and god does the time fly. Seasons are changing outside the window. Fall turns to winter, like in a movie where calendar pages are flying away. Your pubes go gray.

When I finish with this spirited session, I'm immediately disgusted with myself. I'm in my refractory period, thinking, "Never again. What's wrong with you? You could have invented something in that two hours! You'll never get that time back! And that girl is probably a runaway. That's somebody's daughter. You sicken me." So I angrily grab the mouse, click the browser closed and *pow*!

This is my computer. My desktop background picture used to be one of my cars, but when I wasn't paying attention my wife swapped it for a picture of the kids.

Believe me, she knew what she was doing. I'm sure this shot was staged. I can hear Lynette coaching them, "Natalia, could you look a little more disgusted? And, Sonny, go ahead and laugh a little bit harder at what a loser Daddy is." It's as if they're trying to say, "It's a miracle we're even here with all the beating off you do. What did Mommy do, go to the hamper and squeeze out a tube sock?"

Let me try to end on a more positive note. This one involves another bathroom interruption but, this time, there was a nice ending. I had gotten up early one morning to do a bunch of radio interviews. In between, I sipped on my coffee and munched on a fiber bar. Well, of course, the bowels got moving, so I plopped down on the toilet. I didn't bother to close the door, as it was just me and the kids at home, no nannies or maids to bust in.

The bathroom I'm referring to is small and windowless. Thinking I was alone, and just popping in for a quickie, I left the door ajar about a foot and a half. Partway through my deuce dropping, boom-boom, out goes the light. (Bonus points to anyone who got the Pat Travers reference there.)

Someone had walked past the bathroom, flipped off the light and kept walking, wordless. I quickly did the math and yelled out, "Sonny, did you shut off the light?" He said, "Oh, were you in there? I'm sorry." I did a quick wipe, stood up and walked out of the bathroom. I reached for him, choking up a bit, "Don't you ever apologize to me for that," and squeezed him like he was a tube of toothpaste. I'm constantly railing about the wasted electricity in my home and he had proven, with one flip of a switch, that he actually listens to me. It was a great moment. I've never been so proud of him or so happy to have my rare alone time on the throne of my castle interrupted.

CHAPTER 3

☞ Don't Be This Guy

AS THIS BOOK is filled with advice for my kids, I'd like to take a little time to list the people that I hope they don't grow up to be. Kids, pay attention. I'm laying down a preemptive disownment if you become this guy or gal.

First Up: Sonny Boy's List of Don'ts

Zombie Guy: Not naming names, but one of the guys that I employ took a ration of shit from me one day because he was wearing an *Evil Dead* T-shirt.

I just don't get the fascination with the undead. We're all undead. Big deal. And I feel like any one of us could outrun a zombie. They don't run; they don't even jog. They shuffle. It's like being scared of the eighty-four-year-old guy dragging his oxygen tank through a casino.

It feels like there are a hundred shows and a million movies about zombies. Are we not satisfied with this topic? I keep seeing shit about the zombie apocalypse. I'm pretty sure we have a military that could handle that situation. A bunch of decomposing guys ambling toward you, mumbling "brains," aren't going to be much match for an M1 Abrams tank.

I haven't seen *Evil Dead,* so it's not an issue with that specific movie. It is the fact that this dude is in his early forties. How are we so out of problems that forty-three-year-old educated men can be obsessed with the undead? I've long complained about adult males who are into this nerd fantasy bullshit, whether it's zombies, comic books, *Game of Thrones,* whatever. When did it become okay for guys to start talking about how much they were anticipating the *Silver Surfer* movie, and how devastated they were when it didn't live up to their expectations? We all have computers with porno and Wikipedia. You could become an expert on something in a weekend. Do it.

Foreskin Restoration Guy: Sorry for the cock talk, son, but if you end up as one of these assholes, I'll know I did a shitty job as dad. Because that's what this whole deal boils down to. If you complain about your foreskin, it is just another way of saying, "I hate you, Dad." We did have you circumcised mostly for the hygiene aspect, otherwise you'd have to pull that banana peel back and do a little extra cleaning. Plus, I was hoping that you'd play a skill position on the football team, and every ounce of weight you can cut counts.

For some bizarre reason, out here in California there is a movement to ban circumcision. It should not be shocking to you that this movement is centered around ultra-liberal places like San Francisco and Santa Monica. And there are guys who go through various surgeries and attach weights and insert balloons to supposedly restore their foreskin. That's a lot of calories burned just to freak out your next hooker. I know that uncut is natural, but it just looks weird. It's like a Doberman with floppy ears. That's how God created them, but they look fucked up.

These guys always make a big stink about supposedly being mutilated. I'm pretty sure we've been doing this for thousands of years. Heck, it's a sacred rite in Jewish culture. Which is why they all become agents: They're used to taking ten percent off the top. Half the world is cut and the other half is uncut, and it hasn't made a shit bit of difference. So, Sonny, if you're making a big deal about your now smaller penis, that means you're just pissed at me about something else. You've picked a cause to pour that anger into. This is not an issue. This one we should file under "Who gives a fuck?" Don't be one of those dicks who has to make it about their dick.

Formerly Fat Guy: I think you'll have a good metabolism like your mom, Sonny, and this shouldn't be an issue, but, just in case, if you do gain a bunch of weight, just stay that way until you have your massive coronary.

Tom Arnold came up on the podcast recently, and I saw a picture of his now skinny ass. I didn't like it. We need to get the word out to all the formerly fat people that if they're planning on getting skinny, we're not into it. We know you as the fat guy first. No matter what your nationality is, what your job is, what your sexual proclivities are, fat trumps all. To us you're just the *fat* Asian guy, or the *fat* guy in accounts payable, or the *fat* gay dude.

And, personally, I like fat guys, because they make me feel better about myself. When you get into it with a fat guy you always win. If a cop writes you a chicken-shit ticket, and you look in the rear-view mirror and see him waddle back to his cruiser, you can think, "I win, because you're a lard ass and I'm not." If a guy swipes the spot you were trying to park in at the Costco, and he gets out of the car and you see that he's a wide load there to get a pallet of Chef Boyardee, you can think, "I win, Tubby, even though I'm here to buy Rogaine and wine." Even if the guy is getting out of a Bentley in front of a salon in Beverly Hills and you're in a Daihatsu Charade, you can still think, "I win," as you watch him waddle in for his weekly pedicure in elastic waist pants.

What former fatties forget about, especially the guys, is that you don't go from fat to skinny in our eyes, you go from fat to weird. We don't understand you anymore. That was your identity. We were all thrown off for a year like when Jonah Hill lost all that weight. And don't even get me started on what's become of Al Sharpton. Al, get back in your velour tracksuit with the giant medallion and jog on over to Roscoe's Chicken and Waffles, we miss you.

Weird Handshake Guy: Sonny, one of the signs of being a real man is having a real handshake. A nice firm grip that says, "It was a pleasure doing business with you." So don't become one of those guys who has a limp handshake, for God's sake.

We've all experienced this. We go for the shake and it's like the Pope holding out his hand for you to kiss his ring. Are you afraid that you're gonna have a big meeting with some Japanese businessmen later and want to save your grip?

There are lots of variants on the lame handshake. There's the guy who grips the front of your hand and just milks your cuticles. Or the guy who has an odd style of handshake. I don't mean the soul brother complicated eight-stage handshake. I'm talking about the guy who takes the traditional handshake but instead of going up and down he goes right to left, or who takes your hand and turns it ninety degrees so that it is flat, and then shakes. People won't think, "It is nice doing business with you," if you go in with a handshake like this. They will think, "Too bad he was bullied as a child," instead.

Empty Ice-Cube Tray in the Freezer Guy: I know this seems a little specific, but it is time to focus on the tuned-out fuck at your office, or God forbid, your home, who is too ignorant of other people and so wrapped in their own thoughts that they can pull off a move like leaving an empty ice-cube tray in the freezer. I have encountered this in my own studio. One of the lackeys used up all the ice and couldn't take the 8.34 seconds it takes to pour some water into the tray before putting it back in the freezer so that when the bossman wants to toss a couple cubes in his Coke, they're ready. You know you took the last one, you can feel the weight difference as you slide the empty tray back in. This is like putting an empty toilet-paper tube back on the holder. These are the same assholes who don't put the tin foil back on the tray of food at the staff lunch, so that the flies can shit on the roast beef. It's not that they forget—it's that they don't give a crap.

Then there is the dick who leaves the microwave door open. The microwave at our studio is a constant issue for me. Not only do people leave the door open for the light bulb to burn some extra kilowatts for no fucking reason, they'll leave time on there, too. If you take your shit out of the microwave early, just zero it out so that I don't have to deal with it. I shit you not, I put a cup of coffee in the microwave and went to hit start and some asshole had left it at 3:31. What the fuck were you microwaving that you could take it out and still have over three minutes left, a buffalo? And why didn't you zero it out? Enjoy that 3:31, whoever you are, because once I get to the bottom of this, that's how long you have left under my employment.

Anti-Milk Guy: Speaking of food and drink, there is another jag-off that I hope my son never becomes. The anti-milk guy. It's nearly 2020 and we're still arguing about milk. We all know the idiots who say, "We're the only animal that drinks another animal's milk." These are the same Whole Foods ass-Wholes who say, "People weren't meant to eat meat." Then why do I have incisors, numbnuts? Those fang teeth we all have evolved for the pure purpose of tearing at meat.

These idiots also say, "We're the only mammal that drinks milk into adulthood." Here's what I have to say to all those mammalian motherfuckers. I don't see any manatees inventing Facebook. Maybe they would if they started drinking some other mammals' milk into adulthood. I'm going to gather all of these dickwads in San Francisco (and many of them wouldn't have a long commute to get there), park the Space Shuttle on the Golden Gate Bridge and say, "Hey, bitches, any other mammals come up with this shit? No? Then shut the fuck up and drink some milk."

Unfinished Beer Guy: I can't tell you how many times I've had a party on a Saturday night, and then walk around for an hour on Sunday morning, tearfully emptying 2,600 unfinished beers. I feel like the guys who removed the bodies from a Civil War battlefield. Where's the honor? You're not supposed to leave a wounded man behind. Who is the asshole that grabs a cold beer the host of the party paid for, cracks it, takes one-and-a-half sips, then sets it down without a coaster to sweat and leave a ring on their Steinway? How is this okay? Are you that much of a puss, or did you start the beer right before the Feds busted in, and you had to jump out the window? This is far worse than the guy who has too many and pukes into the potted plant. I'd much rather you be the asshole who finishes his beer and passes out with a lampshade on his head than the one who can't finish that last three ounces of Michelob Ultra. Make your old man proud, Sonny boy.

Next Up: Natalia's No Nos

Breastfeeding Activist: The female version of the anticircumcision crusader is the breastfeeding activist. Yes, breastfeeding is natural and important. It's not the act that bothers me. It's the *enormous* deal made about the act. When it comes time to breastfeed find a nice corner and a blanket, and take care of business. Don't be the chick who wants to sit on top of the player piano in the mall and breastfeed in full view, and then lawyers up and sues when someone asks you to go to a less public space. For you breastfeeding blowhards, this isn't about breastfeeding at all. It's about you calling attention to yourself. You could feed your baby anywhere, but you choose high noon at the Vatican so when someone says put a blanket over it you can alert the media. Urinating is also completely natural and important, but if I took a leak into the fountain at the Bellagio, I'd be zip-tied and thrown in a Vegas jail cell (again).

It's like the guy with the aggressive piercings and facial tattoos that gives you the "What the fuck are you looking at?" when you stare. Mission accomplished. You're angry, so you do something to get yourself judged, and then you get angry about being judged. There's a way for you to breastfeed without drawing attention to yourself, lactivists. You choose to do it publicly and make a crusade out of it to make it about you. Do I need to see tits every time I go to Foot Locker? I just don't know why these breastfeeding activists need to shove their titties down my throat. (Actually . . . I'm turning the corner on this one.)

Half-Marathon Chick: I'm not a big fan of the marathon, and the people who need to prove something to themselves and get that picture with the tin-foil poncho being put over them at the finish line, but whatever. What I really don't like is the way the marathon shuts down the city. It's even worse when it's a half-marathon. Everyone reading this could complete a half-marathon. If your car broke down 13.1 miles from civilization, do you think you'd just impale yourself on the hood ornament? No, you'd just walk that half-marathon. A lot of people doing the half-marathon are walking it anyway. To them, I ask, would you brag to someone that you climbed half of Mount Everest, or that you were playing hoops and you went to the one-and-a-half point stripe and drained one, or that you grabbed half a boobie? If you have something to prove, lock yourself in your apartment and don't take a shit for two days. That's way more impressive.

So, Natalia, if you become one of those ladies with the "13.1" bumper sticker on your Subaru please drive it 13.1 miles away from me and never look back.

Drunk Woman Who Calls Herself a MILF or Cougar: The rise of the terms *MILF* and *cougar* has given drunken older broads carte blanche to continue being loud and annoying way past the point at which we guys would tolerate it. The twenty-two-year-old chick dancing on a table at the bar can be an annoying twat as long as she wants, because we're all hoping that, in the midst of that annoyance, she'll lift her top. But when it's the forty-two-year-old, we're not interested, just irritated. But because her appletini-drinking desperate housewife friends have enabled her by calling her a *cougar,* we all have to deal with her nonsense. Now that she's a MILF or a cougar, she feels okay acting trashy. If we all just called her what she really is, "Mom," she'd slow down pretty fucking quick.

Slow Crosswalker: I was in San Francisco, running a little bit late for a live show. And I had the slacker chick in the crosswalk in front of our car with her face buried in her phone, texting. She was walking so slowly that she was literally leaning backward. She looked like a weatherman reporting from a category 6 hurricane. Have you ever seen those people who are walking so slow that their feet are a yard in front of them? I thought, "Bitch, are you trying to get run over? Because this is what you'd do if that was your goal."

Then I thought about it on a bigger scale. People in general don't cross the street well anymore. It used to be a sprint, followed by a shoulder roll, then pop up to finish the sprint and stick the landing on the sidewalk. Because when we were kids, people had horrible old drum brakes, and were drunk, so the chances of you getting clipped by a Buick were pretty good, if you weren't hustling. Nowadays, people aren't frightened. They're not scared.

Here's my solution. I think that everyone between the ages of seven and ten should get clipped by a car just once. I'm not saying run over by a dump truck and put in a coma, just enough to give them the proper amount of fear for the rest of their life. Like the person who gets bitten by a dog at age three, and then is scared of them into adulthood. Parents: Just put your kid in the driveway sometime around second grade, back into them and, when they're writhing in pain with their femur coming out of their ass, you say, "Doesn't feel good, does it? Sure would hate for that to happen again." They need a healthy respect for the automobile. It's going to save their lives and it's going to save me time.

This may not be too much of an issue for you, Natalia, being a honky and all. This slow-crosswalking is the domain of the brothers. I think it's a subtle revenge for slavery and racism. As if to say, "I'm taking my time, Whitey." I've always found it ironic as I watch the big brother amble across the street, that the world's fastest men are the world's slowest pedestrians.

Past Life Regression Chick: Natalia, let me just tell you, this is your one go around. You've never had a past life. If you decide, at a certain point, that you must have been someone in a past life, rest assured that in this life you'll be a chick without a dad.

I'm always amazed at the gullibility of the ladies (though some guys do it, too) who are into this past life regression nonsense. These charlatans are just telling you what you want to hear to make you feel better about your loser life. Sure, you're a fat chick strung out on painkillers now, but a few hundred years ago you were Joan of Arc. Feel better? That will be seventy-five dollars. Ever notice that past life regression only seems to go back five hundred years? What about the fifty thousand we spent as cavemen? It's always, "You were a knight during the Crusades" or "You were a poet in ancient Rome." It's never, "You were just some hairy asshole eating bark until you froze to death."

And, finally . . .

Complicated Starbucks Order Chick: I was behind one of these clowns not too long ago, and the order was so inane and complicated I had to run to buy a notepad, just so I could write it down and make fun of her on the podcast. She ordered a "grande skinny vanilla latte, light foam, extra hot." Let's break that down. Grande. It's a fucking medium. Just say medium. Skinny. I'm sure the skim milk instead of regular and fake cancer-causing sugar is going to make a fucking difference when you try to squeeze your ass into those yoga pants. Vanilla. If you really want vanilla, go to McDonald's and get a shake. Coffee is supposed to be coffee. Light foam? Do you like foam or don't you? You'd need a fucking microscope to tell the difference between the regular amount of foam and light foam. And "extra hot." How does that even work? Coffee is as hot as it is. Extra hot just means undrinkable for longer. So am I, as the next coffee orderer going to burn my tongue when I get a cup of the scorching batch they made for you because you need to make a spectacle of yourself?

Let's take a look at the bigger picture. This was attention-seeking behavior. If I hadn't been behind this chick, if she were alone in that Starbucks, she would have ordered a medium black coffee and called it a day. But because there were witnesses, she had to make her order as long as the Magna Carta. Asking for "light foam" and "extra hot" is just a way of complicating things so that there's one more thing the lowly barista can screw up for her highness to complain about.

These retards are retarding the process. Congratulations, bitch, you've successfully slowed down everyone else's life to make it about you. You don't love foam, you love *you*. I opened the door to the place and hit someone in the ass due to the line you caused, because the poor Starbucks kid is now heating up Bunsen burners and putting shit in centrifuges so that you can have your perfect cup of coffee. It's not even coffee anymore. Starbucks is diabolical. Calorically, what this pretentious bitch was ordering is probably as bad as a Blizzard from Dairy Queen, but they've called it a coffee, so she gets to feel like she's not just buying and consuming a hot milkshake. This is also bullying the person behind the counter. You're lording your power over the poor tattooed teen.

There should be two lines, one for regular people like me who just want a caffeine delivery system. There would be a sign reading "Normal" above it. In that line, you can only order coffee and, when you do, it's just called a medium, and you put the milk and sugar in yourself. Then there would be another line with a sign above it reading "Poser Douche," for the assholes who want to order the seasonal macchiato, light foam, extra hot, with soy milk, easy on the nutmeg.

I hope you kids have taken this warning to heart and will avoid becoming any of these assholes. But with my luck, Natalia, you're convinced that you used to be Cleopatra and are reading this right now at a Starbucks, sipping on a skinny peppermint mochaccino with soy milk while Sonny, who used to be fat, but is now thin, is listening to it on audiobook while he runs a half-marathon to benefit "survivors" of circumcision.

CHAPTER 4

☞ Hey, Kids, Here's a Note to Your Future Therapists

I KNOW THAT all the shit I'm talking about the twins is going to be used against me at some point, so I want to take some time to set the record straight on a couple of things that they'll surely bring up to their future therapists. I'm going to address this directly to you, guy with suede patches on his elbows, and Jewish broad with the dream catcher on the wall.

First, I've done therapy myself, so I know how this works. And I respect it. Ironically, I come from a family of therapists. My grandmother was a sex therapist who worked for the VA and once famously asked at the dinner table what a rim job was, because one of her vets had brought it up in group that day. My dad became a therapist back in the 1990s. He had been reading self-help and philosophy books my whole childhood anyway (instead of coming to my football games), and eventually decided to go pro.

And, to his credit, when I was nineteen, he sat me down and pretty much said, "You're going to be a mess. Your mother is a disaster, I'm a train wreck; you're going to need some therapy." I was making seven bucks an hour digging ditches at the time, so he said he was going to find me a therapist, and that it was going to be a woman so I could work on my mom issues and that he would pay for half and I'd pay for the other half. For someone making minimum wage coming up with even half of the seventy or eighty dollars an hour for a decent therapist was rough. But it was worth it.

To all of you reading this who are on the fence about therapy because of the cost: It's smart money, spend it. That one hundred bucks an hour pays off down the road when you learn through therapy how to get out of your own way, stop self-sabotaging and thus make good decisions about relationships and career. Think of it as an investment in yourself. Simply going to therapy helps. Just carving out an hour for yourself, and deciding that you and your life are worth spending some time and money on makes a difference. That simple act alone boosts your self-esteem. Don't think of going to therapy as "I'm a broken pile of crap and need someone to fix me," think of it as "I'm going to change myself for the better instead of crying, masturbating and blaming my parents for the rest of my life."

So, back to blaming my parents. I was such a broken pile of crap from my childhood, therapy was inevitable. I've done all kinds of therapy: individual, couples and group. Group therapy is kind of rough, especially when you want to leave the group and there's resistance. Once, when I tried to leave my group therapy, a chick confronted me, telling me I was in denial about how bad I was and that I needed to stay. I think it was her issue, really, some dad shit she needed to work out that she was putting on me. Group therapy is like having all the baggage that comes with a relationship with a crazy chick without the spirited crazy chick sex.

I've also done regular one-on-one individual therapy and appreciated the experience, though I don't love it when a group of therapists share an office. It's uncomfortable when you see another person sitting in the waiting room and start wondering what their issue is while attempting to avoid eye contact. Especially if you have regular appointments, you see the same guy every week and can hear him in the next room. Seriously, I've heard shit coming through the vent system I will never unhear. I've heard "My father wouldn't stop raping me . . ." while I'm sitting there complaining about my Lamborghini. Makes me realize that most of my issues fall squarely into that rich white people problems category.

I've also done the couples counseling thing, which I didn't like much. But I still think it works, just not in the way it's supposed to. The reason couples counseling is effective is because you have to report to someone, typically a woman, who is siding with your woman about how horrible you are. At least that was the case with me. I've had people tell me that couples therapy worked for them and saved their relationship. For me, it was just a probation officer that I had to report to. So on Tuesday, when she comes home and wants to unload about her boss and you grunt, walk past her, holding a sandwich on the way back to your *Duck Dynasty* marathon, knowing you have couples counseling on Friday forces you to turn around and listen. It's like mandatory drug testing in the workplace. It doesn't make people not want to do drugs, it just makes people understand and avoid the consequences.

I do think psychology is important. We don't put enough emphasis on this as a society. We live in a civilization, we live amongst other humans, but we don't really know how they tick. If we lived among lowland gorillas, we'd study what makes them happy or what enrages them and their mating rituals, so that we could live in harmony with them. But we don't do that with other humans. Instead, we live in a world full of PSAs for click-it-or-ticket and motorboat safety. You see the president coming out of church on Sunday, and you realize he probably doesn't believe it but he has to do it because, if not, he'd be unelectable. But that same supposed Christian president would be unelectable if we found out he was seeing a shrink, which I think is bullshit. I want the guy making the most important decisions for the country to have an idea of the forces that influence his choices, the ramifications of his fucked-up childhood on his thinking and how that affects all of us. Imagine how much better our country would be if Nixon, Clinton and W. had gotten some real good therapy. So I respect you, Mr. or Ms. Shrink, and the work you're doing to undo the damage I've done to my kids, but let me set the record straight on a couple of things.

First off, I never laid a hand on them. How could I be an absentee father and an abusive father at the same time? Even if I thought I could beat my kids, that would require me to be at home instead of onstage in Portland . . . though I was able to Skype in some emotional abuse from the road.

Of course, I'm joking. But the truth is hitting my kids is just not in my wiring. If you grow up in Hawaii, you eat poi. I've never touched that shit. So I don't miss it. If I were a native islander, I'd miss it on the mainland. Same with child abuse. The idea of me hitting my kids is not on the menu. I didn't grow up with it, so it's not an option. As far as I'm concerned, the thought doesn't even occur to me. One evening, after skipping my rope, I was trying to pound out forty push-ups like usual. I had my Beats headphones on and was cranking the Graham Parker. I had my eyes closed, and was totally in the zone. Out of nowhere, Natalia ripped the headphones off my head and wailed like a banshee in my face. I was startled. Had it been my buddy Ray, he absolutely would have gotten punched. But in that twentieth of a second, I processed the face of my daughter and that was no longer an option.

I know that, as a therapist, you're on the same page, but allow me to rant a bit about this topic. There are certain cultures for whom this is a big issue, and there are cultures around those cultures that suffer the damage. Sometimes, the issue of corporal punishment becomes a national conversation, like after Minnesota Viking Adrian Peterson got charged with abusing his kid. But it never lasts very long. We make a much bigger deal of someone taking a stick and hitting a dog, than someone taking a so-called switch and hitting their kid. The problem isn't even so much the welts you're leaving on your kid, it's the welts they're going to leave on my kid. Because, by hitting a kid, you're teaching them that violence is the way to resolve conflicts. I know this is going to get me in trouble, but I don't care. Black comedians have this whole "who got whooped harder" thing. It's not a joke; it's a problem. I saw an interview with Michael Jackson's dad, Joe, where the interviewer asked him if he had beaten MJ. Joe said, straightfaced, "No, I never beat him." Then, after a pause, "I whooped him." As if there's a fucking difference.

And speaking of beat, let me take one to talk about Joe Jackson. He's got the hoop earring and the penciled-in mustache. He looks like an evil carnival barker. If there are any Disney animators reading this and you're drawing up a new villain, Google Image some shots of Joe Jackson. The part that I don't get, Joe, is that everyone thinks you're evil and you know you're evil. So why go with the evil guy mustache? Why not throw everyone off the trail and grow the Ned Flanders cookie duster?

When it comes to discipline, I mastered the dad voice. That "Hey!" that stops the kids in their tracks. The Natalia who is sitting on your therapy sofa is probably a lawyer or agent. She was a world-class arguer. Every conversation I had with Natalia was a fourteen-move chess match. It was like a negotiation between the Palestinians and the Israelis. She had this toy called an EzyRoller. It's like a mechanics creeper for kids to slide down hills. She loved it. Actually, if she isn't a lawyer or agent she's probably ended up in the X Games. She freaked me out with this thing. I'd be screaming as she luged down a forty-five-degree grade. She'd be screaming, too, but with delight. One night, she announced she was going out with Olga and would be bringing the EzyRoller with her. It was already dark and I was afraid she was going to go off a cliff or into a phone pole. So I calmly told her she had to leave the EzyRoller at home. Then she started in. "What if I just drag it with me and don't use it on the hill, just on the flat part." I said no again. "What if Olga holds my hand?" "No." We went through fifteen different variations of this back-and-forth before I had to use the guttural, teeth-gritting, angry dad voice.

She would go 'round and 'round like this with my wife, too. She'd want to take the dog outside, but it would be too cold or too late, and she'd argue with Lynette back and forth for an eternity, until I eventually leaned over the railing and said "Hey! The answer is no. Listen to your mother." We as parents need to stop pretending that we're talking to a colleague at a law firm. We need to *be* firm. These are our kids, not our drinking buddies. It is okay to be harsh and lay down the law once in a while.

Natalia could take your last nerve and work it like Sugar Ray Robinson working a speed-bag. We had a nice go 'round about a

Actual note from Natalia's door (cross-out courtesy of Sonny)

trip to the American Girl doll store just recently. She wanted to go, I told her I had to work that night and the one in Hollywood was too far away. She told me to go online and see if there was one in the Pasadena area, since it was closer to home. I actually did that, and there wasn't. The closest one was in Glendale, which was nearer than Hollywood, but still too far to make it back on time for me to get to work. Before I knew it, she had dragged me into the later rounds. I was punchy and was playing her game. So I said, "Daddy has to work tonight, but we can go next weekend." She said "But . . ." and knowing I was on my heels and she could knock me out with one good emotional haymaker, I jumped in with, "I said no and the answer is no."

Of course, she then went and told Lynette who sat me down later to say, "When you raise your voice to Natalia, it upsets her." I told Lynette I've only done it four times in Natalia's eight years on the planet. Lynette paused and said, "True . . . but it really upsets her." To which I replied, "Yes, but she plays us both like a fucking fiddle and I'm sure she's telling you this so you'll give me a talking-to so I won't do it anymore, but every time I have raised my voice it has been justified." So if she can manipulate Mom, I'm sure that, as her therapist, you're hearing a lot about her dad the rage-aholic, too. To set the record straight, I've shouted at her maybe four times in the first eight years of her life. That's twice per presidential term. Hardly abuse.

It wasn't just Natalia, Sonny got in on the action, too, in terms of destroying Daddy's will to live. A few years ago, we were having a Super Bowl party and I attempted to enlist the kids to help prep the house a little bit. I had a big cooler in the courtyard, an old-style Coca-Cola cooler like you'd see in a country store. We had a bunch of old sodas in there that needed to be taken out so that we could put some fresh beers in. So I asked the kids to clean it out. It became a more protracted argument than *Roe v. Wade*. It was like I had asked them to drag their own crucifix up a mountain before I nailed them on it. They fought me at every turn. I had to break it down step by step, "Open the cooler, take them out, put them on the table." "But, Dad, they're sharp." There were no broken bottles or cut-up cans. I wasn't asking them to dip their hands in broken glass, like in *Kickboxer*. I just wanted them to take some old faded soda cans out of a cooler. But we went from Super Bowl XLVII to XLVIII by the time we were done arguing, and I had to use the dad voice again. Through clenched teeth, I said, "Just do it because I said so."

Would I love to be able to lay down one well-placed ass whack with a flip-flop? Sure. One flip-flop shot over the bow to let them know that the next step after the dad voice is not going to be good. Instead, I use disappointment as my weapon. Having them in fear of me going out to the backyard and pulling a branch off a tree and whacking them in the ass with it might have gotten me the results I want short term but long term it's going to end with my kids resenting me, and them taking out their anger on society and themselves.

And talking shit about me to you, therapist reading this. But if they fear disappointing me, they'll make good decisions and that momentum will carry them into a good life.

Plus, I don't want the kids taken away. My mom was a product of the system and is still dealing with it, and, in a way, I'm still dealing with it. Having your kids taken away by the government and sent to live in foster care or with relatives does way more damage than any wrong they could do that would warrant them getting "whooped." Again, not pointing fingers at any particular culture, because I don't feel like being called a racist by the *Huffington Post*, but there's a lot of "I was raised by my grandmother" happening in particular communities, and there's also a shitload of crime in those communities. The good news is that immature parents who have their kids taken away were usually raised by young parents themselves. So the grandma those kids end up with usually just celebrated her thirty-first birthday.

Let me say two things about foster kids. First, we need a better name for this. It's too common a last name. There's probably a confusing "Who's on First?" situation on the first day of school for kids whose last name is actually Foster. I think we could come up with a nicer term, like they did when they started calling used cars "pre-owned." Maybe we could swap "foster kid" for "pre-parented."

Second, I'm torn on foster parents. There's a part of me that thinks they are saints for taking in all those kids who need homes. Those kids are usually so emotionally damaged that they end up doing a bunch of literal damage to those foster homes. But, at the same time, I'm slightly suspicious of the kind of person who wants to have a house full of traumatized and abandoned kids. I'm sure there's at the very least some religious proselytizing going on or, at worst, some continued abuse. I have two kids whom I share genes with and

I want to strangle them sometimes. I can't imagine what would happen if some troubled kid whom I met two days ago was in my house messing with my shit and shouting, "You're not my dad!"

Father Abuse

If anything, dear therapist, I was the one who was abused by my kids. That story with the headphones and screaming in my face was not a one-time thing. Natalia always messed with me when I was exercising. One time, I was doing a headstand and she just came in and pushed me over and ran out of the room, laughing, as I came down like a tipped cow.

Our nights of wrestling became more aggressive as she got older, too. Even today, at age eight, we still play the game where Natalia runs off the bed and I catch her. But now, a lot of times, she's pulling some WWE moves on me. As I'm catching her, I'm also catching some elbows to the noggin. One time, I caught her and she just slapped me in the face for no reason. That was when Daddy said, "No mas," and called it a night.

And Natalia tricked me into the abuse. There was a period when, every time I would come home, she'd say, "Daddy, I want a huggy." And of course I'd fall for it. At which point, she'd grab the hat off my head, run squealing into the kitchen, and throw it on top of the upper cabinets. Our kitchen has nine-foot ceilings, but the top of the cabinets are at the eight-foot mark and then there's two inches of crown molding, so once it was up there, it was nearly impossible to retrieve.

This happened multiple times before I laid down the law and said, "You're getting my hat." She stood on top of the counter but couldn't reach, so I put her butt on my shoulder, and she was able to reach back and grab it. She fished it out, showed it to me, giving me just enough time to say thank you, and then tossed it on top of the fridge, which is deeper, so it was even harder to retrieve.

Luckily, this whole thing backfired on her one day. We went through the usual dance of the fake-out hug, her grabbing my Rams beanie and running away. To his credit, Sonny would usually try to stop her, but she'd throw him down and break away like Jim Brown running over a white defensive back. Then I'd try to dive and stop her, but she typically had too much of a head start. On this particular night, she slid on her socks on the wooden kitchen floor, and bonked her head. Then she had that moment all kids have when they fall, that few seconds that feel like forever, when they decide whether they're hurt. So I jumped in and said, "You're fine, you're fine, you're fine. It just made a loud noise."

Then I saw Lynette at the kitchen entrance, making what I call the "Triple Mommy Face." The super-concerned, "Are you okay, sweetie?" look. I was in the middle of my eighty-fifth "You're okay," when Natalia just collapsed in a heap of tears. I swear Lynette and I could have pulled it off if we were on the same page.

Natalia figured out early that it was funny to fuck with me. When she was about fourteen months old she learned to say *no*. And she would shake her head so vigorously when saying no to any request I made that she would fall over. She would hold a ball and when I'd reach for it, she'd pull it back and say "no" so hard she'd literally fall out of her chair. Who taught her this? That's what I want to know. That terrible twos period when kids love to say no is a real burner. It'll take the life out of you. I think all parents should get on the same page and agree not to say "no" in front of their kids until their eleventh birthday. It's part of my campaign: "Just Don't Say No."

Most days, I'm still asleep when the kids go to school. And on those days Sonny would come in and give me a nice kiss on the lips and say, "Goodbye, Father," and head off. (And, for the record, Sonny decided to call me "Father" instead of "Dad" without any prompting or coaching. I have no idea where he got it, but I've gotta admit I love the old-school flair.) Then, moments after Sonny's sweet goodbye, I'd feel a cold flat-palm slap on my forehead from Natalia. She'd seriously just come in and smack me in the head, like I was in a commercial in which I forgot to have a V-8. That's where she was at. Slapping the old man in his sleep.

We actually instituted a points system in the house for doing chores and being good. Five points equals a dollar. So the first time I experienced Natalia giving me an actual kiss goodbye, it was immediately followed by her shouting down the hallway, "That's two points, Mommy. Where's my dollar?"

That one didn't stick. I guess she figured out that it was worth more than a buck to fuck with me. Now when I leave, Sonny gives me the big sloppy kiss on the lips and Natalia leans in, but then slides up to my forehead and laughs.

She's quite the actress. On one of our wrestling nights, she broke down in tears. I thought I had been too rough. But when I went close to check out if she was okay, she punched me in the stomach.

The truth is, she's just not that into me. One night, Lynette popped out to pick up some food. Meanwhile, I was upstairs skipping rope. The kids were downstairs in the kitchen watching television. I wrapped up my rope and walked downstairs into the kitchen. As I turned the corner the floor creaked. Natalia hopped up from her chair, elated, and shouted, "Mommee . . . ughh." A moment of pure, uncut joy followed by a crash of disappointment. Lynette wasn't out of town, she was just out running errands. And in this case Natalia wasn't fucking with me. She was deflated. She was genuinely crushed to see me, instead of Lynette. She wordlessly sat down, turned around and got back to *WaWa Wubzy*.

With Natalia you have to earn her affection. The most she's ever interested in me is when I'm temporarily off the C-list and inching towards the B-list or hanging out with the A-list. She was really into Daddy when he took her to the premiere of *Wreck-It Ralph,* or when she found out that I was doing the *Tonight Show* on the same night as Simon Cowell because she's into One Direction. I'm not fucking around. My relationship with Natalia significantly improved when *Catch a Contractor* started airing. It went from flying beanies and knees in the groin to snuggle time on the couch to watch Daddy on television.

If it seems like I'm beating up on Natalia here, it's because chicks hold grudges and I need to set the record straight. My sister couldn't tell you what century the Civil War took place in or who the first president was, but when it comes to the times my dad ignored her or disapproved of a boyfriend, she's Ken fucking Burns. Girl brains are like computer hard drives that are so full of bad memories and resentment that they can't actually compute. If chicks applied their elephant memory to actual history, rather than the history of the times Dad disappointed them, they'd all have masters' degrees.

I can just imagine the stuff a twenty-eight-year-old Natalia is telling you in therapy. I'm sure I know one of them. My favorite time of the year isn't Christmas; it's the Coronado Speed Festival. That trek 125 miles south of Los Angeles, near San Diego, is my pilgrimage to Mecca. The past two years I took Sonny with me. I made him my pit crew, working on the car together beforehand, letting him do unimportant stuff like hand me tools and spraying down and wiping the fenders with a rag. We drove down together, stayed in the hotel together and even slept in the same bed. It was a real father-son bonding trip. He cherished it and was counting the days to the next one.

For the record, I tried to take Natalia in 2014. I wanted her to have as much fun as Sonny had. She didn't want to go. I'm pretty sure she said *no* just to fuck with me. Anyway, Sonny will be telling his therapist, "Father worked very hard and would always try to make time for me." Meanwhile, Natalia will be saying, "That asshole was never home, he was always working and when he did have time he would spend it with Sonny."

I know it probably feels like I'm doing an unfair amount of complaining about Natalia, but the reality is that Sonny was just easier to deal with as a kid. I've always said Natalia was like raising three kids, while Sonny was like raising one old cat. She was just more energetic and she drove Sonny nuts, too. He was like a Labrador trying to take a nap and she was a caffeinated Chihuahua bouncing around nipping on his ears.

In fact, for this book, I did a little memory refreshing and listened to the radio show from the couple days around their birth. Two days after they were born I said, "The boy is a little quieter than the girl . . . it could all change . . . but at this point the boy is a little quieter." It never changed.

Natalia was always more active and was the first to walk, at just eleven months old. She was long, lean and graceful, while Sonny was shaped like a butt plug. I remember she balanced herself on the edge of the couch, then took three or four tentative steps while holding the cushions before falling into my arms. But if I stood too far she wouldn't go to me, and if I were too close, she wouldn't bother. Enter the string cheese. There isn't a person or a creature on the planet that doesn't love string cheese. Even dogs love it. Someone with full-blown leprosy could hand me a piece of string cheese and I'd eat it. I thought this would be a good motivator and gave her a taste. Then I stepped back three paces from the sofa. Reaching out for the string cheese, she kept going and quickly put together a full twenty steps. I was so proud of my little girl. Not only did she have Daddy's sense of balance, she wasn't even a year old and understood how capitalism works. (Or at least drug dealing. "Here's a taste, but the rest will cost you.") But while I was tempting Natalia with mozzarella, Sonny was just rolling around crapping himself. So I knew, early and often, that Natalia was going to be more energetic and thus harder to handle.

That could be a good thing. I'm glad she has a motor. It didn't make for an easy parenting experience, but it probably means a bright future for my little girl. Maybe Sonny's a deadbeat asshole on government assistance now, and Natalia is a multitasking millionaire philanthropist opening schools for girls in Darfur.

And, credit where credit is due, things actually improved quite a bit as Natalia got older. When I wrote this letter, she was eight and I can honestly say that for the past year things have been quite good. I'm sure you, Mr. or Ms. Therapist, know that sometimes the best way to fix a relationship is to ease off a bit. It's like when I do some of my races and I start to go into a skid. The instinct is to grab the wheel and yank it in the opposite direction. The truth is that if you just let go a little bit, the car will pretty much right itself. If you jerk the wheel in the opposite direction, you make things worse. Well, that's what I did to address a lot of the abuse I took from Natalia. I just gave it some space and let her outgrow it. I didn't hover and I didn't shout back. That's an ego thing, a parent struggling for control because they aren't confident. I was. I knew it would get better, and it did.

I love Natalia; I just have to set the record straight because she has a history of misinterpreting or just flat-out lying about Daddy.

For example, after our Lincoln-Douglas debates about the Ezy-Roller, I tried to make it right before she left the house. I came up behind her before she walked out and gave her a hug from behind. She shouted, "You hurt me!" I was just squeezing her from behind and trying to kiss her on the forehead and later she told Lynette I was "choking" her.

One summer afternoon, I took her to the beach in Malibu. This is one of the most beautiful, and thus most expensive, spots on earth. We literally walked past Madonna's and Cher's houses to get to the sand. We were walking around looking at tidal pools and starfish. We spotted a small crab that had been beached and looked like it was struggling. To role model a little humanitarianism, I tried to save the crab. I dumped some bottled water on it to help it get back to the water. But in that process I accidentally turned it over on its back. So I gingerly flipped it right again and sent it on its way.

When we got home that night, I was in the bathroom and I heard Natalia down the hall talking to Lynette and her friend recapping the day. "Daddy found a crab," she said. Lynette replied, "Did he? That's cool." Natalia said back, "Yeah, he killed it." Lynette was horrified. So for the record, I'm not some sociopath who tortures animals. I dumped three bucks worth of Evian on it to save the fucking thing. But I'm sure Natalia's claiming to you that I waterboarded it.

Her most classic lie was much earlier in her life. When the kids were two years old, I'd come home from work and pick them up. I'd grab Sonny and give him a big hug and bounce him around. Then when I would reach for Natalia she would say, "Poo-poos, Daddy," meaning that she had a full diaper or was about to shit herself. It wasn't time to squeeze her like the world's worst toothpaste tube. But after about twenty-six times, I caught on and checked her. Nothing. She had figured out that Daddy doesn't do diapers, and conjured a way to get out of my hugging her.

The Straight Poop About Poop

Since we're on the topic, I know a little about Freud and the whole anal fixation thing and that it's all about potty training. So let me give you the embarrassing details about my kids and their bowels.

First off, kid poop is weird. It's not solid. It looks like you left guacamole out on the counter for three days. Most times. But other times, as was the case with Natalia, it would be these hard, dusty, dry pellets. At a certain point when she was a toddler, her shit looked like something a dung beetle would roll around. I was wondering if she was just eating flour.

When the kids were first born Lynette would say, "You're going to have to change diapers." To which I replied, "Nope, payback's a bitch. I've been busting my ass for the first ten years of our relationship while you've been eating bon-bons. Time to step up." She shot back, "Why, because you're some sort of celebrity?" I said, "Damn straight. I've been celebritying for the past ten years to pay for the house the diapers are in and the in-vitro that made the little shit machines in the first place. I've done my part."

I can count the number of number twos I've cleaned on one hand. I don't have that gene. I'm uncomfortable with the whole process. I don't like seeing my daughter's chest, never mind down in lady-town. You've got to take that wipe and get in there to clean the girl parts. Not happening. And with the boys, you've got to clean around the ding-a-ling and sack. A little kid sack looks like a rabbit's brain or something. It's like trying to clean a golf ball. Shouldn't you just be able to dip them in something? Can't we get My First Bidet out to market?

There were only a few times when I was alone with them when they were babies, so there were only a few diaper-tunities anyway. I remember one night that Lynette was out and it was all me, Mr. Mom. They were crying and I thought, just let them be. I knew I fed them and that they weren't being consumed by sewer rats. But they were unrelenting. I was up and down all night. Sonny used to make a face like a bad Mexican actor before he'd cry, so once I caught on to his tell, I'd blow in his face to confuse him out of it, like a dog hanging his head out the window. It interrupted his thought process and shut down the waterworks. It wasn't effective on Natalia. I had to hang out in their room all night. I couldn't leave or they'd cry. I'd try to sneak out but as soon as they figured out I wasn't around, they'd start wailing again.

Another night, Lynette and the gals were going out to see the Beastie Boys, and before they left I was given the condescending rundown: "Put on the quiet music," "Put on the blankie," "As they nod off, move them from the daybed into the crib." While Lynette was getting ready, Natalia started making noises, like preverbal conversation cooing kind of sounds. Sonny, meanwhile, was crying like a stuck pig. I thought the difference was interesting and funny and wanted to play it on the morning radio show the next day. I grabbed a camera and was videotaping them to capture the audio when Lynette walked in. In full "You idiot" tone, she said, "Why are you videotaping them? Just pick them up." I was already off to a bad start.

While Lynette was listening to the B-boys do "No Sleep Till Brooklyn," the kids had actually gone to sleep on their daybed. I decided that they were both okay and if I attempted to move them to the crib, I'd end up waking them. So I just left them there. Lynette had warned me Natalia would roll around and flop while Sonny would just sit there like a turtle on its back. (A trend that continues today, as far as physical activity.) I figured I'd be fine hopping out of the room for a few to check some car auctions. I was maybe a minute into my second favorite Internet-related activity when I heard some crying. I came back in and Natalia was facedown on the floor. She had rolled herself out of the daybed, two feet down to the carpet. Sonny was still in the bed unfazed. I ran in and grabbed her, she was squealing but seemed more confused than hurt. I checked for damage and was carrying her around, and saying it was okay and not to tell anybody. I didn't hear her hit the ground, just the crying afterward, so I had to assume that it wasn't too bad. Needless to say, when Lynette saw the bump that later appeared on Natalia's head, I was not left alone with them as infants very much.

On a fecal side note: Natalia was a gassy baby. I remember there was one night when she was constantly breaking wind, and then the dog Molly got in on it, too. So I decided, fuck it, I was going to let it fly myself. I was going to fart-icipate. We'd have a nice family fart fest. It was kind of fun, until Lynette came in and blamed me, and then didn't appreciate when I tried to pin it on Natalia and the dog.

When it came time to potty train them, Natalia beat Sonny to the punch. I came home one night, and Lynette said, "Do you notice anything different about Natalia?" I immediately guessed something was up with her hair. That's usually the answer to "Notice anything different?" with the chicks. Lynette told me, "No, she's wearing her underpants." This might seem like I was tuned out, but it's ultimately a good thing that I didn't notice, because the last thing you want is the answer, "Yep, I know that crotch up and down and I noticed instantly something was off." That's what we'd call a *tell* in the *To Catch a Predator* game.

It wasn't a perfect pull-up to potty progression. We developed a system where I had to wake her up at midnight and take her to pee so that she didn't have an accident in bed. It was a little hit and miss. Sometimes she'd beat me to the pee-pee punch. If she was wet, I'd make Lynette handle it. I wasn't fucking with that nonsense. But most times she'd just be in this fog, take care of business and later have no memory of it. I'd rub her head and gently coach her to take a leak, so Daddy could get to bed himself. But I didn't know about the toilet paper part, until I was informed by Lynette that I didn't know that there was front wiping for the ladies after a tinkle. I'm a guy, we only have one use for toilet paper. And I can't wipe for her. That would be super weird. So I'd hand her the paper and let her do it. It was dark, because I didn't want to wake her up and her midnight motor skills weren't so good, so who knows how that all went, but an attempt was made and soon we were all able to go back to bed.

But those minutes waiting for her to pee felt like forever. I'd just sit there and wait in the silence and then, suddenly, it would sound like someone was using a pressure washer to clean the coping of a pool.

MY-DEA

Let me do a little side tangent on bathroom sounds. I was at another one of my vintage races and had the bad luck of having to make a number two in the port-a-potty. I didn't have any other option. That is a fate worse than death. We all know the smell is terrible but what I realized then was that even more disconcerting is the sound. Or lack thereof. The worst noise a man, woman or child can hear is when your ass is on that wafer-thin port-a-potty seat to do a little offloading and the dook doesn't make the splash sound. It just sounds like you shit on a hot rock. That splash noise is comforting, as opposed to that awful "flop" sound. I'd rather hear a dentist's drill. You get this in the airplane bathroom, too. You don't realize how much you miss that sound when you don't have it. This led me to envision another in my series of new apps. I call it *Kerplunk*. You put your earbuds in and, at the appropriate time, hit the button and it plays a nice splash sound, like dropping a charcoal briquette into a bucket of water.

Back to Natalia and her wily urethra. One time, she pulled down the pajamas and underpants like normal, and somehow the stream was off and she ended up soaking her jammies. So I was standing there holding her *pee*-jays, trying not to drip the wee on myself while fishing around in the dark for a clean pair. I ended up grabbing Sonny's Underoos and holding them up to the nightlight to try to figure out what the fuck is going on without waking him up. I was on the verge of just telling her to go to bed without underwear or pajamas. But I didn't want to endure Lynette's wrath if she found Natalia naked the next morning, or the awkwardness of that partially recovered memory. I can just hear Natalia telling you, her therapist, "All I remember is my dad getting me up in the middle of the night, and then waking up naked the next morning."

A couple of times the nightly pee routine did cause some tension with the wife. I came home at midnight once, after two live podcasts in the midst of an incredibly busy week. Lynette was luxuriating in a bathrobe on top of the 1,000 thread-count sheets watching *Homeland*. I literally didn't even know what day it was, I had been so busy. I walked in and told her how burnt-out I was. She agreed that I needed to take a break from the road gigs, and then reminded me it was midnight and that I needed to take Natalia for a piss. I said I was too fucking tired. She said, "You're right." Then added, "Wait an hour, then do it." It wasn't malicious. It was worse. It just didn't occur to her to do it herself. In her defense, when she saw me deflate at her suggestion and nearly pass out from exhaustion, she got the gist and took care of it herself.

As I said, Natalia beat Sonny in the potty-training race. He was still in pull-ups when she had moved on to panties. I tried to create a little quarterback controversy, a little competition and use her as leverage. I started shaming him by calling the pull-ups diapers, which he'd always angrily correct me on.

And a quick tangent on gender roles. One night, we ran out of the Spiderman pull-ups. All we had were Natalia's now no-longer-needed Dora the Explorer ones left. When we attempted to put Sonny in them, it was like trying to put a cat in a crate. He was crying and infuriated that we would even consider putting him in pink girl pull-ups.

Also, when it comes to the Underoos and pull-ups in general,

I don't get it. Aren't you supposed to idolize Doc McStuffins and SpongeBob and whoever the kids' character du jour is? Why would you want to pee on them? Aren't we just training kids to be into weird stuff sexually? We're essentially telling them that if you love someone, you should take a leak on them. This is a golden-shower fetish waiting to happen.

The potty-training issue with Sonny was more about the backside than the front. He was a little obsessed with having a clean butt-hole. So if you, as his therapist, are seeing some OCD behavior that might be why. He would demand that we wipe his butt for a long time, until I made him start to do it himself. We'd go back and forth. He'd be calling from the bathroom, "Daddy, wipe my butt." Then you'd hear me shouting from down the hallway, "Wipe yourself." He wouldn't give up the ass ghost on that one for a long time. He was worried he'd miss a spot. We eventually reached a compromise, where he'd bring me the toilet paper and I'd dust it for dook and make sure he had a clean wipe. I didn't want to do it, but I didn't think shaming my son about his anus was a great plan. That's the kind of thing that will land him in some horrifying porn. So rest assured, therapist, I did my best.

I can think of one pee-related incident with Sonny. There was a weekend when Lynette was going to Chicago to see Bruce Springsteen and taking the kids with her, which meant I got to drive her Audi. After they had been dropped off at the airport, I got a call from Olga but, through a broken cell connection and broken English, all I understood was that there was a problem in the car. I wasn't sure what it was until I looked in the compartment on the passenger-side door. I found a Ziploc bag full of pee. Apparently, on the ride to the airport Sonny just couldn't hold it. I used to be a bed wetter, so I get it. I don't mind the piss in the bag, I just mind the part where it stayed in the car. I called Sonny that night for our usual good-night conversation and tossed in, "And thanks for the gift you left in the car." Not getting the irony Sonny said, "That's not a gift."

So, therapist, I pray that this letter was unnecessary and that their asses have not graced your couch because the sweetness I've seen from Natalia as she's gotten older has continued and Sonny has remained as mellow as ever. But if not, then I hope it cleared up a few of the misconceptions or straight-up lies that you might be hearing in therapy about dear old dad. My wish is that they regard me as firm but fair. But if the twins are in therapy, the one thing I hope they don't say is, "He did his best." That's a tell that you had a shitty dad. It's the lowest grade you can give a parent without completely disowning them as drunken abusive assholes. If either Sonny or Natalia are telling you that I did my best, then all the defending I've done of myself is useless. But, rest assured, if they are at least halfway functioning people it's because every good thing they've said about their mother is completely true.

CHAPTER 5

☞ Punished for Participation

IT ISN'T THAT I don't try to be a good dad. I get involved with their lives to the best of my ability. Sure, I'm not the kind of dad who lets his daughter put makeup on him or gets down on the floor to bust out the gluten-free Play-Doh with his kids. But I do make an effort. It is just that every time I've tried to engage with the kids, it has blown up in my face.

My first mistake was reading to them. I'm not a great reader (which I've, ironically, written about in my other three books), so it's an embarrassing chore. When someone wearing a Curious George onesie is correcting you on your grammar, it's time to take a long hard look in the mirror. I've always been a terrible reader. I was never formally diagnosed with any reading disability. I was tested for dyslexia and passed. It's one of the few tests I wish I had failed. At least that would be an answer as to why I couldn't read the back of a cereal box when I was a kid.

People always said to me, "You must have been dyslexic." I wasn't. Why is it that when a white kid can't read people say he's dyslexic but when a black kid can't read people say he "fell through the cracks." This is a racist thought. I was as white as they come, and I fell through the cracks known as my parents and the Los Angeles school system. That said, Dyslexia would make a great black name. Sounds like a good wide out for the Steelers.

The problem is that I went to a crappy free-range hippie school where we were taught more about hating Nixon than loving the alphabet. Then I spent years doing construction with addicts and idiots and the latest tome from John Irving didn't really come up around the hose that was our water cooler. In fact, on a construction site being educated could be a hindrance. You'd be mocked mercilessly. "Hey, Alex Trebek, why don't you use that giant brain of yours to figure out the nailing schedule on that shear wall."

When I was in the sixth grade, I had to go up to the chalkboard and write the Phys Ed schedule. I had to put the girls in one column and the boys in the other. I spelled girls with a U. *Gurls*. That was the end for me. So reading has always had not just a physical, but an emotional barrier, too. It makes me feel like crap. Thus, reading to my kids was a tough putt. But I powered through. And I'll tell you what I learned. All those years of not reading were worth it. Kids' books are some of the worst pieces of shit ever committed to the page.

One of the books I was tasked with reading to Sonny when he was around five was *Danny and the Dinosaur*.

This piece of shit was written in 1952. You can tell right away, because the kid on the cover is blond and white, as are all of his friends in the book. Today, it would have to be a multicultural rainbow and there'd have to be a kid with leg braces or a wheelchair. But the kids in this book looked like Hitler Youth.

I tried to have a moment and not judge, and just enjoy doing something Sonny liked. Like all little boys, he loved dinosaurs. But I barely made it past the title. It's shitty alliteration. That's the first strike. And it doesn't rhyme. Strike two. Strikes three through twenty-eight were the writing. After Danny rides the dinosaur out of the museum, a dog barks at him. Here's a true quote from the book: "'Bow wow!' said a dog. 'Go away, dog. We are not a car,' said Danny."

I feel like anyone could write that book. You could figure out exactly how long it took to compose by dividing the number of words it contains by the word per minute count of the author's typing test. There is nothing complex or interesting about this story. At all. It would barely count as a first draft.

But buckle up for the big ending. There's a message to be sent. The other children leave and the dinosaur says he has to go back to the museum, but he had a good time with Danny. Danny walks away and goes home. Wow. I'm telling you, that is some *Breaking Bad*–level plot twisting right there. That's not an ending. That's just the place where the author stopping writing. That book ended because the writer needed to take a leak.

The good news is that I don't think Sonny liked it either. But then again, I did read with so much disdain in my voice, I didn't really sell it.

People always tell me not to care about how bad children's books and cartoons are, but kids absorb this stuff. Parents are told that exposing their children to the arts and to classical music helps with brain development. Kids suck up stuff like sponges, right? Would you rather your kids' spongy brains soak up Mozart, or Flo-Rida? Why not go for some higher-quality books while you're at it?

One book I had to read the kids, that did rhyme, was *Who Took the Cookie from the Cookie Jar?* This was one Natalia wanted. They adapted it from a kids' playground song. The first page was the phrase "Who took the cookies from the cookie jar?" repeated three times. Then a skunk spends the next ten pages accusing lizards, mice, raccoons, frogs and other creatures of taking the cookies. Spoiler alert, it turns out it was the ants. But after they get caught, the ants share the cookies. This book goes nowhere and sends a terrible message about theft. So, kids, if you get caught shoplifting a couple iPhone cases, just offer to share them with the mall security guard and everyone will be happy.

Here's the thing that really bothered me about this particular book. I can almost give a pass on shitty writing if the person also illustrated their own story. Okay, maybe you're a hack writer, but at least you can draw. But this book was written by not one, but two people—Bonnie Lass and Philemon Sturges—and illustrated by a third, Ashley Wolff. Is this actually a three-person job? I'm the only one required to make a literal shit; why does it take three people to produce a literary shit?

So my answer to the question "Who took the cookies from the cookie jar?" is WHO GIVES A FUCK?! What was really taken was fifteen minutes from my life that I would like back.

The worst of them all is *Where the Wild Things Are*. This beloved tome has probably sold two zillion copies worldwide over the last forty-five years. Like all parents, I had to read this garbage to my kids. As with all the other kids' books I've been bashing, this is a story about nothing, it goes nowhere and it doesn't even rhyme. Credit where credit is due, the illustration is great, but the words you could write in less than an afternoon.

Those of you who doubt me and wax nostalgic about this book, please read it again and tell me if it's not a pile of shit, or originally written in Hungarian and poorly translated. Because it seems very strange.

And like the ants in the cookie jar book there is a negative message in *Where the Wild Things Are*, too. The kid is being a little shit, even chasing the dog around with a fork, and is thus sent to bed without supper (which, by the way, parents don't get to do anymore. They'd have child protective services called on them). So he's in his room, apparently drops some peyote, floats out the window and goes to a magical place inhabited by some enormous creatures that don't really seem to bother him. They make him their king, but he splits, even though they wanted him to stay and when he gets back from his acid trip his food was waiting for him. Message received. Be a total asshole to your parents, and then abandon your friends. No problem. There won't be any consequences.

Also, like the cookie jar book, it does that cop-out stretch writing thing. It's the literary equivalent of like stepping on cocaine with baby powder. In *Where the Wild Things Are* there are three pages for the following phrases "And he got in his boat and he sailed . . . And sailed . . . And he sailed some more." Is your typewriter broken in a way that only allows you to write that sentence? I'm writing this book. I have a word count from my publishers. I can't just write the same sentence over . . . and over . . . and over . . . and over again.

When I looked up Maurice Sendak's credits I was thoroughly unsurprised to find that he never did a single book for adults. It's not like "Oh, and he also wrote *All the President's Men*."

***

Here's the real problem. Whether it's Mapplethorpe and Piss Christ or a shitty Adam Sandler movie I'm not bringing my family to see it. But I'm forced to read these books. I *have*

This has been going on for centuries. Slightly after the invention of the printing press, parents were being tortured with this tripe. Not that it always has to be published. Nursery rhymes suck, too.

You've got an old woman who lives in a shoe with too many kids and is probably on welfare, babies in cradles falling out of trees, you've got three blind mice having their tails cut off with a butcher's knife and the ring around the rosie song is about the plague.

Then there's Lizzie Borden. We used to take horrible shit and turn it into nursery rhymes. This chick murdered her family. Adorable. That was apparently novel enough to turn it into a nursery rhyme. Unfortunately, something like this happens every day in Dade County. Do we have a Charles Manson nursery rhyme? Are kids on the playground singing nursery rhymes about that chick who drowned her kids in the tub?

It occurred to me one night when I was playing with Sonny's feet how lame the "This Little Piggy" nursery rhyme is. In fact, we shouldn't even call it a nursery rhyme since it doesn't fucking rhyme. *This little piggy went to market, this little piggy stayed home, this little piggy had roast beef, this little piggy had none. And this little piggy went wee wee wee all the way home.* Not even an attempt at a rhyme.

This little ditty first appeared in 1728, well before the Internet. So this piece of shit spread by word of mouth. How did it catch on? There's a weird foot fetish angle to it. I'm convinced that this was "written" by a foot fetish pedophile who wanted to get his neighbors to take their kids' shoes off in front of him. "Hey, I've got this great thing you can say to your kids. But first they need to take their shoes off. Yeah, that's the stuff . . . slower . . . slower."

Also, it is lazy. So the first piggy went to market. Okay, good start. But then the second stayed home? He couldn't go to the carnival or the castle or something? He literally does nothing? The third one had roast beef, which has to be an awkward conversation with the cows he sees at the farm. "How was lunch?" "Good, I ate your brother-in-law." Then the fourth piggy has none. He doesn't eat anything. Creatively, the author just gave up. I want to find this guy and go wee wee wee on his grave.

The funniest part is that I got annoyed by this and decided to hash it out with Lynette, and the conversation got heated. Was the first pig the same as the third pig? We couldn't agree if the first pig went to market *and* got the roast beef. Are there only two piggies? The fifth one went all the way home, is that a different home? Is he coming home to the piggy that stayed home or to another house? Eventually, it got to the point where Lynette was shouting, "He doesn't go back to the other house. He has his own home, you idiot."

Let's Get Physical

I've made it a point to interact with my kids physically. This was something I never got from my parents. When they were just one year old, I was launching them like horseshoes onto a pyramid of pillows on my bed. I knew boys like to wrestle around and roughhouse, but I had figured out by that point that Natalia had the daredevil gene, too. It was in their blood. All my nephews had the gene, too. They had broken arms every other week. All my stupid roof jumping and reckless driving escapades have been detailed in my previous books. So it was inevitable that my kids would have that thrill seeker thing in them, too.

I've already told you about the abuse I take from Natalia during our wrestling matches. Here's the thing—as much as I try to enjoy these moments of physicality with my kids, I always come up short. No matter who wins the match, I'm always the loser.

One night, when they were about four and a half, Olga was in Guatemala taking care of her sick mother. And heaven forbid the wife and I raise the kids by ourselves. So the maid who usually only comes in on Friday had been asked to come in a little extra to help us out. She has a son herself, so she asked if she could bring him. The little boy's name is Nathan. He was six years old.

Well, Nathan had heard about our wrestling time and wanted in. There are three things you should know about this situation before I tell you the story. First, the maid and her man had gotten divorced. I don't know why, I don't speak Spanish and I didn't want to get involved with that telenovela. But I know as a product of divorce how much little boys want to be roughhoused by their old man. So I decided to let Nathan in on the fun.

The second fact is that not only was Nathan older than the twins, he was big for his age. Way bigger than the twins. He had a bucket head and a barrel chest. He was built like a pony keg.

The third thing is that at the time I had a fucked-up knee. I'm a guy who doesn't complain about injuries. Everything else, yes. But when I'm in pain, you won't know it unless it's bad. This was bad. I ended up needing surgery.

Natalia's favorite move at this time was to hop on the bed, take a running start and launch herself at me headfirst. I'd catch her and swing around 360 to throw her back on the bed. Nathan saw this and wanted to try it, too. Again, feeling bad for this kid and his absentee dad, I couldn't tell him to hold back while I wrestled with my privileged white kids. I told him to go for it. It was like getting hit by a train. And since I managed not to get knocked over and toss him back on the bed, he wanted to do it again. I probably wrestled with this king-sized kid for an hour and jacked up my knee even worse than it already was.

Frankly, I'm surprised Lynette even lets me do this. My rough-and-tumble time with the kids has led to a couple of injuries. In fact I started unintentionally injuring them early and often. Over the holidays in 2007, when the kids were about eighteen months old, I was working out with a trainer. We had one of those big yoga balls. He knew I had a great sense of balance and wanted to see if I could kneel on the thing and not keel over. I did it, no problem. Then he wanted to see if I could stand on it. I could. Then he stepped it up and started tossing me a medicine ball to see if I could catch it and still maintain my balance. I could. I was pretty impressed with myself. So the next night, I decided to try and impress Lynette. I was kneeling on the yoga ball maintaining balance when Natalia walked up and quietly said, "Up." I figured if I could catch a medicine ball hurled by a personal trainer and not fall, I could pick her up. I leaned down and was able to scoop her up and still stay on my knees on the ball. Then Sonny came waddling in after her. At the time, he was built like a butt plug. He didn't have "up" in his vocabulary yet, so he just stood there staring with an "up" look. So I picked him up, too. Again, no part of me was touching terra firma. I just leaned over and grabbed him and then hoisted him with my other arm. I balanced for a good while with one in each arm while Lynette watched, impressed and getting hot for me. That is, until the phone rang and I unconsciously turned and my knees went out from under me and we all went ass over teakettle. Of course, my instincts kicked in at that time and I protected my greatest treasure . . . my face. That's my money maker. I dropped the kids like two sacks of flour. They both hit the floor with a thud, landing on their backs and heads. Meanwhile, I landed on my chest and looked up from the carpet to see a look on Lynette's face like I had just broken into the house and was wielding a rusty machete. A three-count later, both kids exploded in tears and Lynette scooped them up. They were okay. But then again, it's hard to tell when a kid might be concussed. It's not like they have big presentations to make the following morning. Their next day was crapping themselves and being fed oatmeal, which is what usually happens when you have a traumatic brain injury, anyway.

We had recurring dance parties, too. Every now and again, I'll fire up iTunes or Pandora and just dance with the kids. (As my long-time fans know, the only time I feel alive is when I dance.) We'll just crank up the Pretenders and rock out. One night, I had my iTunes going and Sonny and I were jamming to John Hiatt's "Pirate Radio." But the next song in the cue was "Dancing Queen" by ABBA. Now, I'm not going to apologize for that. There's room for Swedish pop in the Ace Man's playlist. It was just one of those moments that would have been awkward if someone walked in to see me and my seven-year-old son dancing and singing along like a couple of drunken bridesmaids. It's like the time I was at the kids' school to build a haunted house with the other dads. I was kind of the foreman since I had the most experience. I wasn't a dick about it, but I did lob in a few condescending comments towards the other Hollywood dads with their fourteen-volt cordless Black & Decker drills. (If you're asking yourself now why they deserve to get made fun of for that, please lump yourself in with that pussy lot.)

I figured we should have some music going while we worked, so I pulled my car around, and turned up the '70s channel on the satellite radio. The first tune to come up was one of the few Eagles songs I like, "New Kid in Town." But I still felt the need to announce that I put it on the '70s channel and that this wasn't my iPod. Thank God I did, because as I was giving the speech Helen Reddy's "I Am

Woman" started. Like ABBA, I have a place for this song in my repertoire, too, but it's not exactly construction site music. You couldn't hit me with a little Foghat? How about some Edgar Winter, seventies station? We're building a haunted house; would it kill you to pump a little "Frankenstein"?

 When it comes to music mixes like Songza and Pandora, we've got to get our playlists straightened out. The whole Songza theme playlist for waking up with energy on a Sunday morning, throwing a summer barbecue and so on, has one fatal flaw. Shortly after I moved to my current home, I was out playing ball with the kids in the backyard and enjoying myself for a few moments. I went back into the kitchen where Lynette was listening to "Penny Lane" by the Beatles. I said to her, "I love this song. Do that thing where you get it out on the speakers in the backyard." So as I walked down the hall toward the backyard, she hit a couple of buttons to pump it out of the speakers out there. And as I stepped out, I heard the last seven seconds of "Penny Lane," and it went right into John Cougar Mellencamp's "Hurts So Good." Without breaking stride I turned around, marched back in and told Lynette to change that piece of crap.

Who likes both those songs? I don't know one person that enjoys the simple beauty of "Penny Lane" *and* the sonic cat-o'-nine-tails that is "Hurts So Good." When that song comes on at the pizza joint and you're forced, for those horrifying three minutes, to listen to it, it's like you've done something wrong. So what kind of maniac is putting this list together? It's musical whiplash. You're going from one of the best songs ever written to one of the worst ever recorded without some sort of buffer song.

I'm going to invent an app that inserts those buffer songs into predetermined playlists, so if the playlist builder felt some Satanic urge to include "Hurts So Good" after a classic and make my ears hurt so bad, the computer will override it and jam something mediocre into the mix so I don't get the bends. This way, as you're listening to music it's not like getting plucked out of a Jacuzzi and shoved into a snowbank. And the definitive not-great-but-not-terrible buffer song is "Main Street." Which is why I'm naming the app Seegr.

Coach Carolla

Both of my kids are involved in sports. Some of which I approve, others I think are a waste of time and are going to turn my kids into pussies and prima donnas. But the bottom line is that all of them cost me time, money and a little bit of my soul. Don't get me wrong, I love seeing my kids having fun and succeeding, but the other parents, the bureaucracy and the everyone's-a-winner bullshit make me want to forfeit as a father.

I'll start with the parents.

Maybe it's because I'm in Los Angeles, but I've had an assful of "cool" parents. The ones who put their kids in T-shirts of bands they listened to when they were younger. I sincerely doubt that your fourteen-month-old is really into Motorhead or Run DMC. This is you jacking off, hoping someone else at the soccer game will tell you that you're cool. But it just shows that you're desperate. Sonny had a Tiger Scout event that I attended recently, and I saw that the forty-something dad who was serving as the Scout leader was wearing slip-on Vans. He was wearing the same shoes as Sonny. I'm not saying that the guy has to sport a pocket watch and monocle, but there should be a little distinction between adult and kid. When you're in a position of authority, the black-and-white checkered slip-on canvas shoes do not scream *leader*. Also, it's pretty ironic that the guy leading a group of kids who earn merit badges for knot tying was sporting shoes with no laces.

One place that was rife with hipster parents was the Hollywood YMCA. I was the assistant coach for Sonny's basketball team there. First off, the Hollywood Y should be called the Hollywood Why? It's a weird place. If you ever want to see a homeless guy on an elliptical machine, a dude working out in jeans and flip-flops or a chick dragging her dog behind her on the treadmill, that's the place. But I had to visit that village of the damned and attempt being an involved father.

Sonny is a pretty good basketball player. He's lean and quick but he's not aggressive at all. He can run down the court but he doesn't try to get the rebound. He's not hungry for the ball. I told him one day, "You know my nickname for you? The Vegetarian Cheetah. You're fast but you're not hungry." He said, "I like it." I don't think he got how insulting it was supposed to be.

Anyway, his games started at eight-fifteen in the goddamn morning, and the other dads were packed into their skinny jeans and their hair was perfectly unkempt. Clearly, there was a ton of effort being made attempting to look like no effort was being made.

And these same parents abuse their kids in an effort to make them as cool as they think they are. One of the kids on Sonny's team was a blond boy with super-long hair. He looked like Kate Hudson's androgynous kid. The poor coach could never figure out if this kid was a boy or girl. Because the kid is six, you kinda have to go off the hair to ID the gender. It was so wildly uncomfortable watching him talk to the parents about their kid, as he squirmed to keep it gender neutral. This is such a narcissistic thing on the part of the parent. You're giving the kid a gender-identity disorder so that you can feel cool. He doesn't need a look. He's not trying to get laid. He's not launching a line of hair-care products. Just let him be a six-year-old boy or her be a six-year-old girl and stop making it about you, Mom and Dad.

These are the same parents who give their kids the so-called unique names I wrote about earlier. One week, I was leaving the Y with Sonny and heard behind me a mother shout, I shit you not, "Coltrane! Coltrane!" I silently prayed that she was black, so I could give her a pass. Nope, skinny blond in yoga pants. Ugh.

I was the assistant coach of Sonny's team, but one week I was flying solo. And boy, was I bitten by the unique name snake. I didn't know any of his teammates' names. You know me, I don't sweat the details. Plus, I had missed the last two practices and had been traveling during the past two games. So I had everyone gather 'round and give me their names and jersey numbers, because a coach has to yell at players. There are substitutions to be made and whatnot and you don't want to shout, "Hey, half-breed, you go in for future lesbian." I made the mistake of expecting normal names like Mike. Because that's how you remember names, you associate them with other names in your life. I work with five guys named Mike, so that would be an easy name for me to remember. I've got a couple of Kevins in my life; Jimmy's son is named Kevin, so I could hang on to that one. So I got on one knee, called everyone in and said, "I need everyone's name." And here are the names, there are no alterations and I've not added or exaggerated for comic effect: Hudson, Declan, Devon, Finn, Harper, Jenson, Reese and Dash. Not one real name in the bunch. Are there no more guys in America under twenty-five named Doug? How am I supposed to remember Finn and Dash? Not a Mike or Kevin in the whole group. I ended up doing a lot of "Hey, Jew-fro, get back on defense."

Two things made this event even worse. First, for tipoff of that game the ref called time out and sent Sonny back to the bench and to me, Coach Carolla. He had forgotten to take off his friendship necklace from Jensen. Nothing fills a Dad's heart with pride like your son taking a timeout from his basketball game to remove a necklace from his boyfriend.

Second, the following week I went back to assistant coaching, and a woman of color who was a parent of two of the black kids on the team walked up to me. At first, I thought, *good*, I'm finally going to get my thanks for handling the team when the regular coach was out of town. How naïve! It turns out someone had sent her the clip of me talking about this on my weekly appearance on the Kevin and Bean morning show where I used the term half-breed. She said, "I don't appreciate you referring to my kids as half-breed." I was confused. I said, "First off, half-breed is an Indian thing. Haven't you heard the Cher song?" I even started singing it. She hadn't.

Then she did something that drives me nuts. She said, "Listen, I'm in comedy. So I know humor." That's always a clear sign that the person has absolutely no sense of humor. She worked for TBS or something. I love when people start telling you what a fantastic sense of humor they have before they continue to prove they are humorless twats.

I told her I had said "Jew-fro" and "half-breed" intentionally because there weren't any on the team. I had no idea that her kids were mixed. I thought they were just black. Even if I did know they were mixed I still would have used it. I didn't say mulatto. No one refers to President Obama or Tiger Woods as half-breed. She was so narcissistic she had to make my Cher reference about herself and her kids.

And to all you do-gooders out there who practice the "I thought you should know" bullshit, you're just a grown-up version of the tattletale from sixth grade that we all hated. That person who gives a friend bad news under the guise of "If I were you, I'd want to know" is a special kind of asshole. This is a power trip, a way for you to have dominion over other people's feelings. You get to control them for a minute. Why not knock them down a wrung on the emotional ladder, so they can be as miserable as you are inside? At the same time, you get to elevate yourself by being holier than thou about me, a comedian who's simply trying to get a laugh and actually made efforts to make sure no one's feelings got hurt.

And, by the way, mission accomplished. I no longer coach her kids.

Another thing about all the parents at these events that drives me insane is that they're always taking video of the kids.

In today's culture kids can't go three days without being photographed. I don't know how good it's going to be to have every event captured on iPhones. Family photos used to be an event in and of themselves, dragging the kids down to the Sears portrait studio in ill-fitting shirts and clip-on ties. Taking the photograph was a memory. I see parents now at every one of my kids' events holding iPhones and iPads in front of their faces. It might be fun to look at those videos years down the road. Then again it might be used as "what-happened" footage in the *20/20* episode about them when they kill a bunch of nursing students. But it's definitely bad for the parents. Just be there in the moment, instead of missing it by trying to capture it. That's what your kid really wants. They want you to be paying attention.

Ironically, here's a picture of the team getting a pep talk with Coach Carolla.

And last but never least, the government . . .

Like all things they get involved in, the government fucked this one up, too. Here I was simply trying to spend some time with my boy by coaching his basketball team, and here comes The Man looking over my shoulder.

On the day of Sonny's first practice I signed into the Y, ready to coach like I've never coached before. Because I literally had never coached before. But, I assumed, they're six, they'll figure it out.

Before practice was about to start the woman who worked at the YMCA came up and asked me, "Did you get fingerprinted?" I didn't know what she was talking about, so I said no. She replied, "Well, then you can't coach. You need to be registered and fingerprinted." I started arguing about how that's unnecessary and took one of my many stands in the name of sanity.

This is not a star-trip thing. I just hate that we're removing the part of us that has evolved to have common sense and make decisions. To distinguish between the guy who showed up with his whole family and the guy who showed up solo in the shitty box van. There needs to be some probable cause. If I were a molester or kidnapper, would I bring my wife and other kid with me to the practice? I'm not a pedophile, I've never been a pedophile and thus I don't think I should be treated like a pedophile.

I went back and forth a couple of times until the chick got per-snickety and said, "No prints, no coach," and walked away. Sonny was excited all day for his first practice. He had literally been counting down the minutes. But I needed to make my point. I walked away, too. And when I turned, I got three looks: anger from Lynette, disappointment from Sonny and desperation that said "Don't make me do this alone!" from Coach Mike.

I'd love to say I had a moment of clarity and softened my stubbornness, but that just ain't me. I thought it was more important to make the point. Lynette took matters into her own hands, went over to the bitch with the clipboard and smoothed it over. I managed to assistant coach that day, but then avoided it for weeks in a principled protest against their bullshit policy.

Eventually, I couldn't continue to fight the war on two fronts: against The Man at the Y and against Sonny and Lynette at home; family came first. I caved, drove over to the passport photo/notary public place and got the fingerprints done. And, as expected, it was a colossal pain in the ass.

Because when I say fingerprints, I mean all of them. I still have no idea why they needed all five fingers. Is it like I'm going to take a belt sander to my thumb, just so I can sneak into the Y and molest kids? Can't it just be one finger, so you can connect me to my son? And I say five fingers, but I really mean ten because they need both hands. Because that's what I do, I cut off my arm and rent it out to pedophiles.

I had to press my fingers on this glass-plate scanner, which, like all technology in my life, didn't work properly. We started with the left thumb. But that one didn't take. The Asian chick behind the counter said, "Are you sweaty?" I immediately got defensive, held out my hand and said, "No, touch them." My left ring finger wouldn't take either. I was incensed when the chick said, "We'll get back to it." Yeah, because God forbid we skip one out of ten. It got intimate at a certain point, when she had to hold my hand and roll my thumb. In many countries, we'd be engaged.

At the end of the whole ordeal she printed two copies of the report, one for me to supply to the YMCA and one for me to keep. As I turned to walk out, she said, "Wait, here's your copy." I told her I didn't want it and walked away. I only wanted one for the pussy at the Y who's afraid of getting sued. I don't need pictures of my hands. I'm familiar with them. I know the back of my hands like the back of my hands. What could I possibly discover?

Not to mention, have we started to live for two hundred years? When did time stop mattering? Why do you think I have the time to sit at a fingerprint office, rolling my thumbs and mashing my palms onto glass plates? I resent the loss of time because the government is assuming that we're all pedophiles who just haven't been caught yet.

Natalia plays basketball, too, but her real sport is ice-skating. Now, I know this falls into the white-people problems category, but Natalia's ice-skating unitard cost almost two hundred dollars. And that was half price. When Lynette told me how much it cost, I asked if she got it at the Caesar's Palace gift shop. And that was just the unitard. I don't even want to know how much the skates cost. I think if I find out, I'll use them to slit my wrists.

What was most infuriating is that when I asked Lynette how much the unitard cost, I also asked her where she purchased it. She said she bought it at the skating rink. That's like taking your car to the dealer to get your oil changed or getting hit with the fee at a strip club ATM. Stuff is always most expensive right next to where you use it. (By the way, *unitard* sounds like a mythical special-needs horse.)

I can look at the bright side, though. I am glad that Natalia's into ice-skating and not ballet. When she was three, I warned Lynette that if I saw her taking Natalia to ballet lessons, I would fucking tackle her at the door. Everyone who does ballet ends up as a disaster. They're anorexic, they have body dysmorphia and everyone who teaches ballet is a huge cunt. No one ever said, "My ballet teacher was a delight." They're all the chicks who wanted to be prima ballerinas, but put on a couple of extra pounds, washed out and then took that anger out on your daughter. I'm all for discipline and hard work, but ballet seems like torture.

Natalia got into skating early. I took her and Sonny roller-skating for the first time in 2011. She was definitely better at skating than he was. Sonny was like a Keystone Kop. He couldn't keep his feet under him at all. He was like a Stooge and the whole floor was banana peels. Natalia did pretty well right off the bat. I think she got Daddy's balance, though she did need to use my arm as a support, like a chin-up bar. This was a little tough on the torn meniscus I had at the time.

But like all attempts at joining in an activity with my kids, some asshole adult had to ruin said activity for me. We were at your standard-issue roller rink so of course there was shitty tween music to contend with. The tunes were to be expected, and were therefore tolerated. I knew Katy Perry and Taylor Swift were going to be on the playlist. I didn't imagine I was going to hit the roller rink and be treated to a rock block of Dave Edmunds, Joe Jackson and Elvis Costello.

What drove me nuts was not the music, but the DJ. It was a female DJ. I think that, when you graduate DJ school, there's two lines: one for all the guys that says "Future Strip Club DJs," and one for the gals that says "Future Roller Rink DJs."

She did a couple things that outraged me. First, she made an announcement as we were circling the rink that the next song would be for "couples and people who want to go solo only." Isn't that all human beings? Unless there's some special polygamist skate, couples and individuals encompasses everyone on the planet.

That was just confusing, but not enraging. Then there was, "The next four songs are all request." As if she wasn't going to just play the same Hilary Duff song she intended to play, and pretend someone requested it. I'm pretty sure if I got up there to ask for "Burn" by Deep Purple, that request would not have been honored.

The thing that really got under my skin was when she announced that it was time to play that special four-square game and told everyone to choose a corner if you wanted to play. And if you didn't, then it was time to leave the rink.

Well, the kids were still a little shaky and Daddy needed a break, so we shuffled to the opening in the wall, exited the oval, found a bench and sat down. We then sat there as they rolled a big fuzzy three-foot die and slowly eliminated each corner. They'd roll it, it would come up four and she'd proclaim, "Okay, everyone from corner four off the rink." And every time she felt the need to announce, "No new people on the rink." She'd then play another bit of a shitty song, everyone who hadn't been eliminated would circle the bowl and get in a corner before they rolled the die again and kicked out another corner. This went on for about two minutes before I looked at Lynette and said, "What the fuck? Can't we just skate in a circle? We paid. We have to sit here and watch this retarded game of musical chairs without the chairs?" Meanwhile, Natalia was pulling on my sleeve, saying, "Daddy, let's skate," and I was responding, "No, honey, the people have to do their dumb game." Eventually, it was whittled down to a small group, and whatever number the die landed on that corner was the winner. But there was no prize and we were all losers.

Before I had even hit the rink, I had to contend with bullshit policies and the peons making minimum wage to enforce them. I hadn't even set one wheel on the parquet when someone from the rink came over and said, "No hats, sir." I was still wearing a ball cap and hadn't even considered that it would be an issue. I certainly didn't see any signs warning me that this was a no-hat zone. I guess they're afraid it could fly off when I hit the breakneck speed of three miles an hour and someone could trip over it. Thanks, lawyers. Awesome society you've crafted.

The skating rink is an aquarium for people, the human version of the manta rays just going in a circle in that pool at SeaWorld. So when you want to break from the pack, it's an issue. After a few laps, Sonny wanted to get back on Carpet Firma and hit the arcade. But when he decided he was done, we were about twelve feet past the opening in the half-wall circling the rink. So we were faced with a choice: go completely around again, or hug the rail and backtrack. I wasn't going all the way around and Sonny was done. He'd fallen one too many times and was crying. So we went salmon-style up the skating stream. As soon as our skates hit the carpet, the guy from the rink gave me the infuriating "Next time . . ." speech. He had to let me know that what we had done was against policy and that he'd let me get away with it *this time*. Or what? What the fuck are you going to do? Call the skate cops? And, by the way, do you think I'm coming back tomorrow with another set of kids to relaunch my master crime spree? But I bit my tongue. I didn't want to make a scene in front of my kids. It just drives me nuts when peons try to wield their minuscule power. Either let me break your stupid rule or don't, but spare me the "I'll let you get away with it this time but . . ." bullshit.

Then, to top it all off, Lynette lost the rental ticket stub for our skates, so I got to deal with a hassle when I was turning them back in. I tried showing the chick behind the counter the receipt for thirty-eight dollars, which proved we paid for four tickets. Again, I got the "Okay . . . *this time*" speech. As if pilfering used roller skates is my career. "Yes, wily rental-counter girl. I'm an international skate thief. I've run this scam in every town and have a warehouse full of well-worn skates that I put up on eBay. But you've finally caught me. You should sell your story to Hollywood. Think *The Music Man* meets *Zero Dark Thirty*, but instead of Bin Laden and his terrorist underlings, it's me and my skate-stealing cohorts, Al-Skata."

The only fun I had that day was the belly laugh when Lynette was telling the twins about how she went roller-skating all the time when she was young and Natalia asked me, "What kind of roller skates did you have when you were a kid?" Hilarious. Skates? We were lucky we had sneakers. The Carollas' car barely had wheels, never mind our shoes.

So, anyway, now Natalia loves ice-skating. She's done a couple of Christmas skating pageants and even tried out for a production of *The Wizard of Oz* on ice. One day, I ran into Natalia as I was leaving for work. She had just come back from the tryout. She was very excited. She said, "Daddy, I got the part!" I told her I was proud of her as I skimmed through all the possible roles in my mind. Was she Dorothy? Glinda the Good Witch? I guess they could have a girl playing the Tin Man. I asked her which part she landed. She said, "I'm playing the flying cow." I said, "What?" I remembered the flying monkeys, but I didn't remember any flying cow. Lynette clarified that she was in the twister scene, playing the part of a cow getting thrown around by the tornado. My daughter was playing bovine debris. When they write the TiVo description of *The Wizard of Oz*, I'm pretty sure the flying cow doesn't make the cut in the cast list. It was admittedly a failure of parenting when I couldn't help but laugh, crushing her spirits like Dorothy's house on the Wicked Witch.

I'd like to close this chapter on a positive note, showing that sometimes participating in your kids' lives can be worthwhile. Let me tell you about a nice outing I recently had with Sonny. As you know, Sonny and I have enjoyed a few delightful trips to the vintage-car races on Coronado Island. It's always great working on my wheels and bunking up with my boy, but Sonny snores, even though he always denies it the next morning.

I don't understand the guy who denies that he snores. I'm sorry to say that Kimmel is one of them. What do I stand to gain by accusing you of snoring? The whole interaction is uncomfortable. Why would I lie? Do you think I'm a perv that gets some sort of sexual gratification by making people think they have sleep apnea? What kind of sadistic maniac would you have to be to tell someone who lay there motionless all night, like Michael Jackson in the waning moments of his life, when he woke up, "Hey, man, you were snoring last night. I couldn't get any sleep." I said it because it's true. Whether it's snoring, halitosis or the piece of parsley stuck in your teeth, when someone musters the courage to tell you an uncomfortable truth, believe it.

Anyway, whether he wants to believe it or not, Sonny is a snorer. And not an average snorer. Most snoring is rhythmic, so you can eventually tune it out like white noise. Most snoring eventually becomes like living near train tracks; after a while you just stop hearing the rumble. Sonny's snoring had no rhyme or reason to it—it was just startling and definitely prevented Pops Carolla from getting his full eight hours. After one year at Coronado of me dragging ass after a tough night, I ended up buying him Breathe Right strips and they worked like a charm.

This whole event takes place on an active military base, so there are badges and wristbands and all those sorts of things involved. The guy who runs the vintage-race portion of the weekend's events said he could come by and get my signature early, since he would be at the track before us, so we wouldn't have as many hoops to jump through when Sonny and I arrived at the track. But because I had to get up at seven that morning to shoot *Catch a Contractor* in Corona, I couldn't wait for him at home in the morning. So we agreed to meet at six that afternoon, after the shoot. I got home at five-thirty, exhausted as hell and depressed from spending a day in Corona. When you compare Corona, California, to Tijuana, Tijuana gets offended. It's the opposite of a Corona beer commercial. No sandy beaches, just dirt lawns and depressed Mexicans. Adding insult to injury, Sonny and Natalia were on my bed with the vibration mode going as I limped into the bedroom. When I asked Sonny what he had done that day, he replied, "Just chilled." The fact that he chose the word chill, while I was broiling in Corona, really stuck the dagger in.

Anyway, I saw the clock next to the bed and noticed that it was past six and my guy still hadn't shown up. I was getting to the end of my nap window. If I didn't go down now, it would be too late to bother taking a nap. Now I could still grab a good twenty-five, wake up, watch *SportsCenter*, have a beer and get back to bed at a reasonable hour, so I would be able get up at seven the next morning to drive to another hellhole . . . this one called Whittier.

I told Lynette, "I've got a guy coming by to drop off some stuff.

It's six forty-five; he was supposed to be here at six. I'm going to crash. Just tell him to drop off whatever he needs to." I then napped and woke up twenty-five minutes later, as planned. I felt a little bit better, but I still had heatstroke from Corona and was staring down the barrel of another miserable day. And then the pile-on began. Lynette said, "Wouldn't you know it, the second you left the room to nap the guy showed up and rang the buzzer." I asked, "So what do we have, lanyards, wristbands . . . ?" She said, "Nope, he said he needed your signature." Still shaking off the fog of a nap I asked, "But he left the stuff behind to sign?" I'm sure you know where this is headed. Lynette said, "No, he couldn't leave the paperwork, he just took off." Noticing my stunned stare, she said, "I didn't want to wake you up. You said you were exhausted." At first, I was pissed. I wanted to say, "What happened last time you woke me up from a nap, did I throw a samurai sword at your head?" I bit my tongue and internalized my fury. It was my fault, after all. I had spaced on the part that involved me needing to sign the documents. Usually, I just have someone forge my name, but since we were headed to an active military base, it had to be legit. I was devastated. I just wanted to sit and cry. I was just trying to spend some quality time with my kid and take a little break from my crazy work schedule, a guy was offering a way to make that go easier showed up the second my head hit the pillow and was sent packing, thus ensuring that I'd have to do as many laps around the retard racetrack fixing the situation as I would on the actual racetrack. Could it have gone any other way?

Here's how this all connects to my trip with Sonny. Like many of my weekends when I go out to race, I try to piggyback a live gig in the area onto the trip to help defray the costs. This time around, I'd landed a private corporate gig. So I was up late the night before the race. After that Thursday night speech to a room full of suits who'd had too much to drink, I woke up the next morning and Sonny was just sitting on the edge of the bed with earbuds in, playing with his iPad. He wouldn't dream of waking me up. And his Breathe Right strip was sitting on the edge of the nightstand. I asked him why it was there. He said, "It's not sticky anymore, but I wasn't sure if we could use it again." I was filled with pride at his efficiency and cost consciousness.

It was a tight schedule. The day before we had been given a VIP tour of the Jonas Salk institute, then it was on to the corporate gig (I brought Sonny along—I wanted him to see Daddy work). Then on Friday there was a practice race and a qualifying race. I always skip the practice race, but I have to do the qualifying because it determines my starting place for the actual race. But I had gotten a call Tuesday night that week from my agent, James "Babydoll" Dixon. He said he had a gig for me. It was, in agent parlance, "light lifting, and a nice bag," meaning easy money. But it was in Los Angeles, which would mean I'd need to bring Sonny back home before the actual race. I didn't want to ruin our great father-son race weekend, but at the time (and probably even now as you read this book) I owed money to lawyers, plural. I had not one, but two bullshit lawsuits going on at this time. I rationalized the whole thing, thinking that Sonny could come out Thursday, have breakfast Friday morning, do the practice and qualifying race as part of my pit crew, then zoom back to Los Angeles. Sonny wouldn't know the difference between the real and practice race, anyway. But just in case, I asked Babydoll if he could move the gig so I could keep my weekend with the boy intact. Well, he called back two hours later to inform me that whoever had sought me out couldn't move the gig, and when I didn't answer right away, they had gone to someone else. Here's the thing: I needed the money, but needed the experience with my son more.

This was God, the Great Magnet, whatever you want to call it, making a point. I needed to have my quality bonding time with Sonny. I was relieved, to be honest.

Then Dixon called back an hour later saying the other guy had dropped out. So I said count me in. But for those few fleeting moments, I was Father of the Year.

 To Sonny and Natalia, on Buying Your First Car

THIS IS A little note to my offspring, meant to impart some hard-won wisdom on making that most monumental of purchases . . . your first set of wheels. While cars may not be as important to you as they are to me (though they should be), the lessons I include can be applied to any major purchase our kids will have to make one day. Just swap the car for whatever you value—boat, helicopter, NFL franchise. Hopefully they will have the bread to make the purchase without asking us for help, right?

Dear Sonny and Natalia,

Cars were obviously important to your dear old dad and I want them to be important to you. As you know, I had the wrencher gene as a kid, but it was never nurtured. Your grandfather was useless when it came to cars and your grandmother drove a VW Squareback with the engine in the rear under a piece of plywood. Cars were not nearly as important to them as ignoring each other.

Yes, I grew up without something I clearly loved, cars, and have admittedly overcompensated. When it comes to cars, I am like the guy who never gets laid in high school and then when he loses the zits and the Peter Brady voice crack he bangs everything with a pulse. When you're deprived of a passion, you get a hankering for it and, if you can, you'll overcompensate like someone who just got out of prison and walked right into the buffet at the Bellagio.

So I have filled a warehouse with rare and vintage cars, and guess what, you're not getting any of them! I want you to have that hunger, too. I want you to want cars. More important, I don't want you to think that you can get something for nothing. I took you guys to a warehouse full of cars once, and I did not like what I saw, not one bit.

The day after Thanksgiving 2014, I brought you to the garage of my old friend Jay Leno. Do you remember walking around his han-

gar full of more than one hundred and thirty cars? We had to take a golf cart to get around that place it was so big. When we got there, Jay was out in one of his steam-powered cars. He was doing exactly what you'd expect him to be doing, wearing all denim, tooling around in a car from over a century ago that only a millionaire with no kids can afford or have the time to enjoy. He was living up to every stereotypical image you've ever seen of him in tabloids. It was like going to a fat guy's house and finding him on the toilet eating a giant turkey leg. I recall that you kids were pretty bored at first but, eventually, you, Natalia, looked at a car and said, "That's my car, that's what I want to drive to school." It was a Dodge Viper. Among all of Jay's cars this was your first pick. This is a pretty garish and nutty car and at the time it came out, it had the biggest engine you could get in a sports car. The only reason someone would buy this car is to do donuts on their ex's lawn while high on prescription pills. It's all engine and clutch and no backseat. But you had made your taste known.

That's not the part that concerned me; it was what happened next. As we started walking back to the front passing forty acres of cars, you stopped and decided you wanted a different car. You changed your mind. It was like when someone is at the diner, orders the club sandwich but then looks at the table next to them and sees a Reuben, and calls the waitress back to change their order, annoying both the waitress and your dining companion. Your pick this time? A Ford GT.

This will run you about 300K. But then, another 180 yards down, you changed your mind again. You sent the Reuben back and ordered the surf and turf. You pointed at a McLaren P1.

This is a one-and-a-half-million-dollar car. It's not the most valuable car in Jay's collection, some of the older ones are worth far more, but that was the one that had the highest original sticker price. By the time you're in high school and thinking about cars and reading this, that McLaren will be a cool six mil. That's my concern. You have expensive taste. And seeing Daddy's collection, you might have the impression that it's normal to have a couple of Lambos lying around. It's not. Just like all other things in your life that you might desire, I want you to earn it. You, too, Sonny. After Natalia pointed to that McLaren, you jumped in and said, "I'll take one too," like you were ordering a side of hash browns.

So, now that we're a little more realistic about cost, let's think about the future. When you are ready to lay out the cash for your first ride, take a moment to reflect before you sign on the dotted line. Don't get anything too small or too big. I know you, Natalia, you'll want the zippy little car. You have that daredevil gene. You're going to want something cute, fast and sexy, but you're not going to know how to drive it. I knew a girl in high school who had a Triumph Spitfire, a tiny little convertible. I'm a big guy, and the one time I sat in this car, I realized that I could hang my hand out and touch the ground. It has no airbags, crumple zones or anything to offer as far as safety. It's a cute car that a cute sixteen-year-old would surely die in if a big guy with a big Ford F-250 with the lift kit stopped short. Not so cute. You're a rich white girl from the hills, so, statistically, this is how you're going to die, anyway. You're not going to get killed in a drive-by, you're going to be killed in a drive-over, when that Ford F-250 smashes you as you're texting behind the wheel. Let's not do anything to stack the deck, shall we? To make sure that you abide by my wishes and stay safe, I have mandated in my will that when I die from exhaustion due to my work schedule your mother implement my safety plan for your first car: a line of tires strung around it like on a tugboat. This is fully legal, and only costs about ten bucks a used tire. Then every six months you go without an accident, we'll take one off.

Now, you might flip the script. You might want to go with something big. You could be that little chick who wants the giant Suburban as a way of overcompensating. We always talk about guys driving big trucks as a way of making up for a small penis. If that's true, why is it that I always see little chicks climbing into giant SUVs? I think it's a power thing. It's the only time when you are in motion with your head more than five feet from the ground. I also think women like bigger cars so they can carry around all their extra shit.

So, Natalia, you're either going to have a small car that is too fast for you or a big car that you can't handle. No matter what happens, I'm sure as you spin your wheels I'll be spinning in my grave.

Either way, you'll need insurance. Though when I see insurance company ads, I'm not sure that insurance is even necessary. I mean, according to these ads, the only time you can get into an accident is if you're having a good time. Crashes only happen if you are having fun with friends, particularly friends of a different race, who are sitting in the backseat. I don't mean driving drunk kind of fun, just jovial, laughing with your ethnically diverse friends kind of fun. And then, *bam*. Next thing you know, you get T-boned by an Escalade. I've never seen a commercial where someone totals their car if they're just going eyes forward, hands on the wheel, with a stern look on their face. When I drive I look miserable and I've never gotten in an accident. Kids, that's my tip. Skip the insurance and drive angry. Hands on the wheel at ten and two, and wear a look like Bill Belichick at a press conference, and you'll never get into a wreck.

Unfortunately, by this time I'm sure there will be a nationwide government mandate on carrying car insurance, so just pick one and get on with your lives. The amount of car insurance commercials currently on television is astounding. I hope it won't get worse once I've departed. You'd think that there was a huge difference between auto insurance companies by how fiercely they compete. But, honestly, they're all pretty much the same. And yet, they keep coming. More and more commercials for more and more companies, all offering basically the same coverage. It's like when they say you spend a third of your life sleeping. This is true. What they don't say is that you'll spend more than half of your waking hours viewing car insurance commercials.

To the insurance company CEOs reading this here's my offer: I'll switch my insurance to the one with the lizard and Lynette's to the one with Flo, if you'll agree to never show those ads again. Deal? Hopefully by the time you kids are reading this, we will have invented a chip you can put into the television that knows you already have insurance, and blocks those ads so you can get on with the business of working to pay for it.

While I'm on automotive innovations, let's talk about car-door openings. Hopefully by the time you're buying your first car, the auto industry will have figured this out. Why is it that when car doors open they only have two settings? It doesn't just flap open like the door on your house, it opens to one place and stops, and then it hops to the next place and stops. The first one is just enough to get a little air in and let a little fart out. It's a crevice just wide enough that maybe DJ Qualls could crawl out of his Denali. The next place car doors stop is where it slams into the door of the Camry next to you in the Best Buy parking lot. That opening is wide enough for the guy from *The Blind Side* to step out of comfortably holding two bags of groceries. It's either too open, or not open enough.

Hey, car manufacturers, how about a nice middle ground? A Goldilocks zone, where I can get out comfortably without denting the car next to me? What's that first opening for? "Hey, I need to let my ferret out to pee?" Not only that, but all the parking spots are getting smaller and all the cars are getting bigger. Plus, our fat asses are getting bigger, too. This is a disaster. Statistics I just made up show that this opening issue is the reason for the 92 percent increase in car-door dings. All I'm saying is let's treat car doors like a vagina, we don't want it so tight we can't slide in, but also not so wide you feel like a tube sock alone in a dryer.

Anyway, on to you, Sonny, and your first wheels. Don't get anything too cool. A lot of cops are car guys. They were dudes who loved cars and took the cop gig so that they could do burn-outs, and maybe get into a high-speed chase. So, as car guys, cops will be quick to pull over a Lamborghini, just to check it out. You want something nondescript that blends in to get around this. One of my good friends intentionally drives a Volvo station wagon so that he won't get pulled over. That guy has pretty much circumnavigated the globe while tipsy, and has never once been pulled over because he drives the official vehicle of upper-middle-class soccer moms. So, Sonny boy, take a booze-soaked page from his playbook. (I don't want to get him in trouble by naming him, so I will keep this alcoholic anonymous.)

Speaking of getting pulled over. Let Pops give you both a couple of tips on getting out of a ticket. Natalia, you're going to be a good-looking young woman, so you should be fine flirting your way out of a ticket. Sonny, you'll be in tougher shape. You'll be a handsome young man, too, but the number of gay male cops who will let you off when you flash your pearly whites is going to be pretty tiny, and any female cops who pull you over will probably be more interested in Natalia, if you know what I mean.

I don't know if you guys recall, but back in 2014 I actually got pulled over with both of you in the backseat. I had not been pulled over in seven years, thanks to my radar detector keeping me aware of all the spots where the cops hang out at the bottom of hills, waiting to pounce. Plus, I always drove with one eye in the rear-view mirror. Not the safest move, but in Los Angeles you have to drive scared.

On this particular day, we were driving to the ocean. In an attempt to avoid a traffic snarl, I made a last-second decision to hop off one freeway and onto another. I sped up to hit the off ramp and instantly saw a California Highway Patrol cruiser in my rear view. He didn't have his radar going, so my detector hadn't gone off. I was just a target of opportunity. My usual cop Spidey-sense let me down. He hit the rollers and pulled me over. I was doing eighty.

By the way, the top speed on the car we were driving was 177 miles per hour. I hadn't done anything unsafe. The most dangerous thing about the whole scenario was him pulling me over and getting out of his car to walk to my driver's side window. He was much more likely to get clipped after he got out of his cruiser than any potential

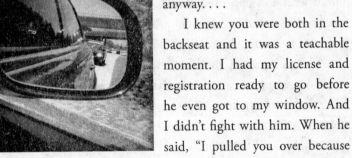

accident I could have caused. But anyway. . . .

I knew you were both in the backseat and it was a teachable moment. I had my license and registration ready to go before he even got to my window. And I didn't fight with him. When he said, "I pulled you over because you were going eighty," I didn't shoot back, "Come on, it couldn't have been more than seventy-three." I just said, "I understand." When he asked for a reason, I told him the truth, "I was going on one ramp and changed my mind at the last second and just kind of blanked."

The first thing I knew was that this cop hadn't been lying in wait with a radar gun. Those guys are ticket-writing machines. They exist to write tickets; that's their mandate. So if you get hit with one of those quota-meeting assholes, you're getting a ticket, no matter how you react. I knew I was just low-hanging fruit for this guy, and thus had a chance to sweet talk my way out of it. That's the lesson, if you start arguing or give a bunch of excuses, cops are going to give you the ticket just to prove the point. If you push back, they'll make sure you know who's in charge. Make them not want to give you a ticket. Make them feel bad for doing their job.

It worked. He let me off with a warning, and we then sped well over the limit all the way to the beach. It wasn't because I was a celebrity; the guy didn't recognize me. It was because I was a cop-killer with kindness. I hope you will always remember this little nugget of wisdom.

But just in case you have too many brushes with the po-po, here's another tip. I once got pulled over on Van Nuys Boulevard doing seventy-five in a thirty-five miles per hour zone. Obviously, I knew I was way over the limit, and that there was no wiggle room. I fully expected a ticket. When the cop started asking me all the usual questions, he threw in an extra one I wasn't expecting: "Where'd you get that hat?" I forgot that I was wearing an LAPD hat that someone had given me. It was just a coincidence. But being quick on my feet, I told him, in my best humble-brag tone, "I do a little charity work for the boys in blue." I'd probably done one celebrity golf tournament, and was shitfaced the whole time, but I didn't go into details. He walked to his motorcycle for a minute, then came back and let me off with a warning.

So here's the tip, a tip of the cap so to speak. Travel with baseball caps for the police department of every municipality in your area. Do what you have to do to get your hands on them. Go to the local precinct, and say you have a sick kid who loves the cops or something, and then put them in a box in your backseat and swap them as you cross county lines.

While we're on caps, here's a great idea that I never got around to manufacturing. Take this and run with it, kids. This simple device will help you and all drivers avoid tickets while using the HOV lane.

To be honest, I fly solo in the HOV all the time. You have to in Los Angeles, if you want to get anywhere. What I do is lean the passenger seat back, and pull the shade down on the passenger's side, like the sun is bothering Granny's cataracts. I'll even pretend to be talking to that person: "Grandma, all the kind words you had about my car headliner have been nullified by your hurtful comment about my double chin."

It's simple, just two hooks that clip over the passenger side headrest, attached to a baseball cap. That way, cops coming up from behind think that there's someone tall in the passenger seat. It'll have a drape of black velvet coming down the back so you can't see through that space at the bottom of the headrest. It'll just look like you're commuting with Yao Ming. If you get pulled over, it's not technically illegal and sometimes cops have a sense of humor. Or they'll pepper spray your ass. But it's worth a shot, right?

I'm sorry I'm not going to be around to teach you how to drive, Natalia. I would like the challenge. I know saying this in print will further paint me as the misogynist ape that a lot of people think I am, but chicks can't drive. I don't let your mother drive when we go out together unless I'm drunk. Which is often.

On my short-lived Speed Channel show, we did a bit where the other hosts and I had to teach models to drive stick shifts in high-performance cars. I ended up with a ditzy actress in a Dodge Viper. This thing has 600 horsepower, 650 foot-pounds of torque and a super-hard clutch. It's a grizzly bear, the last of the muscle cars. I was in the passenger seat, and I didn't want to end up crashing through a mall like the Blues Brothers so I knew I had to make sure my lessons got through. The first thing people do when they learn to drive stick is let the clutch out too quickly without giving the car enough gas. So I said to this chick, "Give me a safe word. Something I can say to remind you to put the clutch in." She said, "Voltaire." I have no idea where that came from. So I told her "When I say Voltaire, take your left foot and push it to the floor." Lo and behold, the plan actually worked. Saying "Voltaire" over and over got pretty annoying after a while, but it proved that if I could teach her to drive a manual transmission, I could teach anyone.

Not that I would get the chance if I were alive. I lament that you kids, and kids in general, aren't ever going to drive manual cars. We were much more engaged behind the wheel when we drove stick. There's no texting and driving with a manual transmission. You have to focus, but you feel totally in control, too.

This is especially going to be a handicap for boys. Therefore, I am making this deathbed proclamation. Sonny, you must learn to drive stick. Being able to downshift and blow around another driver, to bump start a car, and the simple satisfaction that comes with you jiggling the stick in the right to left to make sure it's in neutral, are all rites of passage for a young man. It makes me sad to think that you'll probably have a car that not only doesn't have a manual transmission, but has back-up cameras and can parallel park itself. I've made my wish clear. I hope out of respect for your dearly departed dad you'll . . . *stick* to it. (Good stuff, Ace Man.)

I want to reiterate the most important feeling I have about you two and cars: I'm not buying one for either of you. A car is something you have to earn. All of my shit vehicles were detailed in my previous books: trucks with bolted-down bar stools for seats, screwdrivers for keys and vice grips replacing the missing window cranks.

In Carolla style, both of you are going to have to go through a series of shitboxes, like I did, so that you can feel the pride of ownership that comes with a new vehicle. I want you to feel the sting of driving a car with a coat hanger for an antenna and a tampon string holding the tailpipe in place. I want you driving the car I saw recently in Long Beach. It was a seven-year-old Toyota with duct tape holding the rear taillight in place, that was so sun-blasted that the silver had worn off. The light was being held by the white cloth skeleton of the duct tape. It was so sad. That tape had been in place for at least two years. When the duct tape cries *uncle,* when the tape taps out, you know you're driving a piece of shit.

What killed me about this particular vehicle was the "Toyota of Long Beach" license-plate frame. You know, the cheap plastic plate frame they put on every vehicle that leaves the lot? It's a good idea at first, it's free advertising. But a couple of years down the road, when it's adjacent to the duct-tape gauze holding the car together does it really scream, "Come on down to our dealership"? If I were Toyota of Long Beach, I'd set up a system so I could size up the buyer of the car before I let them drive off the lot. If the person is wearing flip-flops and a mustard-stained sweatshirt and is trading in a Tercel with partially eaten In-N-Out Burger in the backseat, he's getting a plate frame for one of my competitors' dealerships, like "Toyota of Gardena."

Remember kids, your car becomes you. If you have a disorganized mind, you'll have a disorganized car. Poking your head into someone's vehicle tells you everything you need to know about them. It's like the Hickory Farms sample at the mall. When you get the taste of that summer sausage on the toothpick, you don't need to eat the whole thing. You know what you're getting. When you look in someone's car and they've got spent scratch tickets in the passenger seat and a basket of dirty laundry in the backseat, you know exactly who that person is.

That's why I'm not into hand-me-down cars. I've seen the young male driving the totally cherry Lincoln. That just means Nana died. No young dude would pick that car. And that spells disaster for that Continental. Because it was a hand-me-down, that guy is going to drive that shit into the ground, literally. Nana kept that thing in tip-top shape until she kicked off, but once her jackoff grandson gets hold of it, the cloth interior will be pockmarked with cigarette burns, the suspension will be shot from going seventy over speed bumps and doing brodies in the grocery store parking lot at night and it'll smell like Willie Nelson's hair.

When you don't earn it, you don't care about it. If I bought you each a brand-new fully loaded Mini Cooper when you turned sixteen, that car would be covered with fast-food wrappers on the inside and bird shit on the outside within a month. Meanwhile, the kid who busted his ass working two afterschool jobs slinging the fries that you then drop in your gratis car will be treating his like a Fabergé infant. He'll attend to that thing in every spare moment he has, and spend every extra dollar he has on maintaining it. This isn't a dig on you, Natalia or Sonny, this is human nature.

Let me bookend the chapter with a tale about why car ownership is so important to your old man.

Sonny, in 2011, you and I had a nice father-son trip to Orchard Supply Hardware, followed by a little wrenching. We walked around the store for an hour and a half, and Papa loaded up on paint, nuts, bolts and other odds and ends. You were very patient. Then we went back to the shop and wrenched. I gave you a Phillips head screwdriver and you pulled a panel off the door of one of my lightweight Datsun roadsters, all by yourself. It was great.

This was also incredibly symbolic. I hope what I am about to say shames not just my family, but all families. As a culture, we understand that when a young boy wants to play a musical instrument, we get them some drums. Or when a young girl wants to design clothes, we buy them some fabric, needles and thread and let them go to town. I'm sure a young Vera Wang was making little dresses for her Barbies. Well, early and often, I had an inclination for wrenching, but this went ignored. My parents were too busy being depressed faux intellectuals to attempt caring about something as blue collar as cars. Let me ask you this: If a kid showed a penchant for playing the violin and you didn't encourage that, you'd be considered a monster, right? Well, what about the kid who wants to tinker with cars? It's the same thing. We've just decided as a society that tools are for meatheads and cellos are for smart people. Some of the brightest guys I know are car guys—it takes a mind to understand mechanics. In our society, you could be the big brain from the DC think tank who comes up with the solution to getting us off foreign oil, but not know how to change your own oil. So who's smarter?

The point is, it was torture having no garage and a lame dad. It was so fucking pathetic and infuriating that we did actually have a garage but instead of it containing a car and tools, it contained my mattress and was my bedroom. I wasn't going to do that to you, Sonny. But I wasn't going to foist it on you, either. You can't force that.

So as you read this, if you're leasing a Camry and GPS-ing directions to the nearest Jiffy Lube that's okay; I gave it a shot. But I'd be damned if I wasn't going to give you the *opportunity* to activate that part of your brain and see if you were a born grease monkey, like your old man was and his old man wasn't.

Ultimately, kids, I hope you work hard, save up your dough, pick the right car for you, and, more important, for your race. Let's face it, certain ethnicities prefer certain cars. I actually came up with a show idea around this: *Racial Supermarket Parking Lot Sweepstakes*. Here's how it works. I put ten different cars in a grocery-store parking lot. Then the lucky contestant stands near the automatic doors. I have an easel with foam core cards that read "Asian," "Black," "Mexican," "White," "Gay" and so on. I then hit an air horn and the automatic doors slide open, and the contestant has to run around and put the card on the car that best represents the race. He'll be putting the "Gay" card on the peach-colored Mini Cooper, "Black" on the Escalade with the spinner rims. But the twist is for "Mexican," you have to run off the lot and put it on a bus.

Sorry if that was a little tangential. I just realized I hadn't said anything racist in a few pages, and I don't want you kids to be confused.

Chex Mix to feed them. The kid gets the attention they're missing at home, and the couples who were on the fence get a little taste of parenthood.

___

So, to be honest, I was kind of afraid to have kids because of how [c]luster my parenting was. I waited a long time to reproduce because [wa]sn't sure I was going to take to children. I didn't want to ignore [my] children like I had been ignored. And I wanted to get my career on [trac]k. As an entertainer, a career is very difficult to get on said track. [Ei]ther takes a while or never happens at all. It took me until my [earl]y-to-mid-thirties to get to a point where I felt comfortable that I [coul]d make a living doing comedy, and that I had career momentum. [Als]o felt that I needed more therapy, so I could try to be a little more [nor]mal. So Lynette and I didn't end up having kids until later in life. [And], as such, it took us a long time to conceive the twins.

___

Our in-vitro fertility-clinic saga has been well documented. I'd like to make an observation about the rise of this in our culture. Almost everybody I know had to go the fertility-clinic route to have their kid. All the guys had to do the thing where they go into the little room and jack off into the cup using the well-worn porn provided by the clinic. It recently occurred to me that there's now a whole generation of kids who were conceived while their fathers were looking at a woman who isn't their mom. When they get old enough to ask where they came from, we're going to have to sit down and tell them in a heartfelt tone, "When a mommy and a daddy love each other very much, the daddy pays thirty-five thousand dollars and goes to the bathroom of a place in Encino that used to sell flooring and watches Ron Jeremy do Jenna Jameson in the ass."

CHAPTER 7

☞ What I Learned from My Parents by Not Learning from My Parents

A QUICK SPOILER alert for my parents: If you're reading this, just skip this chapter; you'll be offended.

Who the fuck am I kidding? They didn't read my last three books, why buck the trend?

A few years back, I was in a store with my dad. Coincidentally, I was on the cover of *Wired* magazine that month. My dad noticed it in the store, picked it up, glanced at it for a second and then, without a word, put it back down. I was mere feet away from him and he never uttered, "When did this come out?" or "Hey, did you see this?" or anything at all. He picked up that magazine, looked at it as if Tony Hawk was on the cover, and moved on.

So if my folks are breaking with tradition, reading this and are offended, well, they rolled the dice. They thought at best I'd be talking shit about them to day laborers on a construction site. They never imagined I'd have millions of listeners to absorb my vitriol about them. I've called my dad a pussy and my mom a basket case a hundred and twenty-seven thousand times on the radio and podcasts. Why change now?

Besides, I'm writing this for you, my fellow parents, who still have the chance to improve. My mom and dad's parenting skills were DOA.

As you know from my previous literary efforts, I was raised like a hamster. My parents just put some wood shavings on the floor and shut the door, and I walked around in a circle until my eighteenth birthday.

They're not bad people; they're just not into family. Ironically, family is not in their DNA. My dad had two brothers that I never met. It wasn't like there was some Italian family feud going back to the old country. He didn't have a beef with them, as far as I know. It's just that a bus ticket or a long-distance phone call costs money. His dad had died when he was a teen, so he never had a real relationship with him. And, as I've spoken about many times, my mother was raised by her grandparents, due to a situation I'm still not clear on, but involved child protective services. This went on until she was ten and moved back in with her mom, my grandmother. Until then, she thought her mom was just a family friend who stopped by on occasion. Again, I'm not sure of all the details, but I guess at some point, my grandmother just popped out with, "Oh, and by the way, I'm actually your mother." As a result, my mom for her whole life called my grandmother by her first name, Helen. It was like how Bart Simpson calls his dad Homer. It was never Mom, it was Helen. That

should tell you everything you need to know about how the trickle-down emotional economics worked i

It's kind of surprising that my parents had kids know, I could have been an accident. I never asked going to. I think that most likely my parents though child, but then realized they didn't want everything t it. Kind of like how a kid wants a puppy, but doesn up all the pee and poop.

One thing my parents did do was lower the bar If my parents can do it, then *anybody* can. We're so n it comes to child rearing. Don't give yourselves too m ents. By the time you finish this sentence twenty tho have been crapped out. The majority of them are go fine. A few are going to be abused and end up as addi are going to settle into standard-issue, unnoticed, sub to all the potential parents out there, stop getting u You can do this. If you're on the fence about having That indecisiveness means that you're at least giving i before you actually create a human being, and wil enough of a shit to parent pretty well. It's the people sider whether they should have kids who shouldn't. the ones for whom a child is just the thing that hap blow your wad and move on to fucking another Flori

 My brilliant plan to keep these morons from ing is this: a kid petting zoo. Parents tha middling can drop their kids off all day an bucks, the couples who aren't sure if th to be parents can come in and pet the kids a little (n ual way). They can toss around a couple Nerf balls around in a little red wagon and, for a quarter, get

Getting out of my family's negative cycle and having kids has been rewarding on a number of levels, but also frustrating—not just from the stuff I've been talking about in previous chapters, but also because of the context. Knowing how much I enjoy spending time with the twins makes me hate my parents even more. Speaking of context . . .

The Carolla Bunch

Growing up in the '60s and '70s with my parents was rough, especially when I'd watch television. That was the era of *The Brady Bunch* and *The Partridge Family*. I'd sit on the floor and watch these shows in which happy families all hashed out their problems and had great bonding moments in a half hour every week. Meanwhile, my sister had run away, and my parents lived in separate rooms, thinking of ways to kill themselves and end the misery. My house was a chaotic, filthy mess, with sofas covered in sheets and people who didn't talk to each other. The Bradys would have Alice the maid (another luxury they had that the Carollas could never have imagined) call everyone down for dinner and the happy kids would run down and sit around the table.

Then we'd have little Bobby Brady in his plaid sweater, staring blankly ahead, playing with his food. Inevitably, someone would ask, "What's wrong?" This made me irate because not only was no one in my family tuned in enough to notice that I was bummed the fuck out, I didn't even have the Salisbury steak and mashed potatoes to move around with a fork. This is such a fake scene. That would not happen in real life. As depressed as I was, there was no way I would have pushed away any food and said, "I guess I'm just not hungry." I would have buried all of my feelings in food. If my parents had two potatoes to rub together, I would have been so fucking fat. If being depressed about something was an appetite killer for me, I would have been dead of starvation by the time I was ten. I would have looked like Tom Hanks in *Philadelphia*.

And on the subject of *Brady Bunch* style, take a look at the cast from season one to season five. Has anything ever changed so much in a four-to-five-year period? Between season one in 1969 and season five in 1973, everything went from *Lawrence Welk* to *Welcome Back Kotter*. The lapels got wider, the hair got huge and everything went paisley. Robert Reed even jumped a couple years ahead to the disco era and contracted HIV. *Modern Family* is currently on its sixth season. Check out the first season from 2009, and look at it today. Is Phil Dunphy dressed like he's in a completely different decade in a completely different country? Nope. Just one more reason for me to love *Modern Family*, and hate my family for making me watch that garbage.

Anyway, back to the Bradys and their meals. I'd never seen my mom make anything that came out of an oven. I think she was afraid that if she put food in there, it would take up room she needed for her head when she decided to end it all. And my dad didn't even know what a fucking oven was. If you showed him an oven, he'd try to climb in and drive it. I don't even know why we had utensils in my house. I think they were just there in case someone gave in to the urge to start stabbing each other.

This is why I get incensed when I see my kids not appreciating food. It is a trigger for me. This year we took a family day trip to the beach, and when it came time for lunch we went with the sub sandwich plan. Lynette went off to get me a turkey sub and whatever the kids wanted, while I grabbed a table at the food court. She came back and we all sat to eat. A couple of bites in, I noticed Sonny was chowing down on a sandwich from Subway while the rest of us had hoagies from another place. I asked what was up. Lynette told me Sonny preferred Subway. It was a turkey sub, just like I was eating, but for some reason Sonny's had to be from Subway instead of where the rest of us had ordered. It wasn't like the other restaurant didn't have what he wanted. In fact, he got an inferior version.

My real resentment is not about Subway. If Sonny wants to eat crap, that's his loss. It is just that growing up, if I was lucky, I went to one restaurant a year. Meanwhile, my kids go to two restaurants per meal.

Much like entertainment options being too plentiful these days, food options are also way too copious. If you take the kids to the Cheesecake Factory for their birthday, they'll cross into the following birthday by the time they're done reading the menu. That thing is as thick as Oprah's ankles. (By the way, if you want to know why America is fat and our economy is in the shitter, it's because the only factories still in operation have the words Cheesecake and Old Spaghetti in front of them.)

Split Happens

There should be a class-action lawsuit against the 1970s, brought by all the kids whose parents were divorced during those ten years. Like mine.

Don't get me wrong. This was a good thing. They were terrible together. They were the opposite of chocolate and peanut butter. But it's not like there was domestic violence. That would require effort. They chose to beat each other mentally and spiritually with disinterested sighs, disappointed groans and one-thousand-yard stares. It was even worse than physical aggression, they acted like the other was dead and the form walking around our house was a ghost.

So with parents this emotionally disconnected from each other, the divorce was actually a blessing. I have no beef with it. A therapist friend of mine says the only thing worse than divorce is a bad marriage. To all the parents reading this and thinking about divorce, I'd say that in an ideal world, you should try to make it work. But if staying together will cause more damage to your kids than separating, then just rip off the bandage.

But, please, if you decide to split up, consider the timing. There's a window between when the kids are really young and won't remember what happened, and after the ninth grade, when they're going to hate your guts no matter what, when you just have to tough it out. It's your job as a parent to experience some discomfort for the greater good of your child and your community. Stay together between the ages of four and fourteen. Not just for you and for your kid, but for me and my wallet. Unless you want to give me back the tax money I part with to pay for school counselors and social workers to deal with your mess of a kid.

My issue with my parents' divorce wasn't that it happened. It was what they each did after the split. Because it was the '70s when he got divorced, Jim Carolla turned into a regular Bob Guccione. My dad looked like he sold aluminum siding when he was married, but as soon as their marriage was over (I'd argue it never even started), he was rocking platform shoes, a medallion resting on the chest hair you could see because his shirt was undone to the navel and clear non-prescription glasses. He sported a huge Jew-fro, despite the fact that we're not remotely Jewish. I think the most atrocious thing I ever saw him in were jeans that laced up in the front and the rear. It was like a swinging seventies starter pistol went off when the papers were signed, and he decided, "Hey, I'm making the scene. I've got to get laid now that I'm forty-four." He went from Rob Petrie to Phil Spector overnight.

Compare that to my mom.

She packed on about forty pounds and stopped dyeing her hair. So when the roots grew out, it looked like she was wearing a gray Nazi helmet with a tuft of red in the back. She kept the medium-long hair, about shoulder length, but the first seven inches were gray and the rest was red. It was convenient because, like the rings of a tree telling you its age, this was a clear delineation of when she finally gave up. She died on the inside and, ironically, stopped dyeing on the outside.

I think that it says a lot about the nature of men and women that when they split up my mom made herself as unfuckable as possible, while Jim caught Saturday night fever.

At least their breakup was quick. There were no assets, so Dad took his *ass* out of the house and *set* it at my grandparents'. Yes. When my parents split up, my dad had nowhere to crash and ended up at *my mom's* parents' place. What a pathetic cherry on that dysfunctional sundae.

I've got a way to make divorce more palatable. This year I had back-to-back live podcasts in Chicago at a cool venue called Park West. In our Q-and-A segment at the top of each show, we had marriage proposals. That got me thinking about the Kiss Cam that they have at Lakers games at the Staples Center and other big venues. It's mildly amusing to see a couple give each other a smooch on the Jumbotron. But how about this for a plan? Instead of the tired old Kiss Cam, where we get to see you give your wife of twenty-seven years a forced and tepid peck, let's create the Divorce Cam. How much more compelling would that be? The camera zooms in on a couple just as one of them drops the D bomb. Obviously, one party will have had to arrange this in advance with the ballpark. Unfortunately, the other half of the couple will be taken completely by surprise. Then the cam would pan over to the kids who are crying and confused, while the slimy divorce attorney stands behind them with papers and pen. Statistically, half the people in the stadium are going to get divorced anyway; why not use it to provide a little between-innings entertainment? I'd never miss a Dodgers home game if they did this. I bet in the long run, the Divorce Cam would help keep a few marriages intact. It would keep a lot of guys on the straight and narrow because if the wife pops out with, "Hey, the Giants are in town, you want to go to the game?" hubby would be Johnny on the spot with, "Yeah, sure, but not until after I'm done giving you a foot rub and buying you flowers, sweetie."

Life Lessons From Mom and Pop Carolla

As far as life lessons my parents laid out the secret to success: Do the exact opposite of what they did. Like my notoriously bad luck betting on the Super Bowl, where my friends find out who I am going for and bet on the other team, when it comes to fathering decisions I think about whatever my dad would do and go with the opposite. You know those What Would Jesus Do bracelets? WWJD? I have a WWJD bracelet, too, but for me it means What Wouldn't Jim Do? So here are a few of my parenting techniques, thanks to watching the failure of my own mom and dad:

I. DON'T BE CHEAP WITH YOURSELF

I've thoroughly chronicled my family's cheapness over the years: Saturdays spent dumpster diving, decorating a potted rubber plant for Christmas instead of a real tree, having a rolling portable dishwasher. But there's one thing I've never written about that I think is completely symbolic of my family's cheapness, and it is our relationship to Tupperware.

Let me explain. I'm not saying avoid storage containers in general. I hate waste, so I want you to be able to store leftovers. What I'm talking about is hanging on to the container, ironically, past *its* expiration date.

This may not resonate with the younger folk reading this. It seems like Tupperware had the market cornered from 1959 until about two years ago. During this period, it was as if no one else could figure out how to extrude plastic and make a bowl-and-lid combo out of it. Now there are hundreds of brands of disposable containers you buy at the grocery store, use once and leave behind at the party if the guacamole isn't completely eaten. Before this, there were these things called Tupperware parties. Housewives would gather and one of the ladies who had hooked up with the Tupperware Corporation because she was bored now that the kids were off at college would sell them containers. You couldn't get these precious gems at a store. You had to know someone who knows someone and gather under the cloak of darkness.

It's not just Tupperware having a monopoly on snap-lid containers that boggles my mind. I'm still trying to figure out why, for eighty years, there was one and only one blimp. Above every stadium or sporting event since the 1930s has flown the Goodyear blimp. That's all there was. But it seems like somewhere around 2004 we got inundated with new blimps. Now there's the Met Life blimp, the Budweiser blimp, the Fujitsu blimp . . .

Blimp technology hasn't changed that much. It's not like Goodyear had a patent on dirigible technology. Why did it take nearly a century for someone to think, "Hey, you know that blimp that's getting all the camera time? We should get one, too." Maybe the Hindenburg got the competitors out of the market.

The Goodyear higher-ups must have been thrilled. "If they just keep running this footage every year, we'll be all set."

It also occurs to me that a blimp is a weird thing to represent a high-performance tire. Blimps move slower than a donkey and use no tires. If everyone drove a blimp, Goodyear would be out of business. Why'd they go with that? This would be like if Jenny Craig's mascot was a manatee.

The point is whether its blimps or Tupperware, I don't know how they fended off the competition for that long. On January first, every year, Bob Tupperware and Roger Goodyear must have gotten up and thought, "I pulled it off. Another year and no one caught on."

The current cornucopia of containers was not the case when I was a kid, and thus provided ample opportunity for the cheapness of my family to come shining through. My grandmother had one piece of Tupperware, which looked like it had been through three tours in Vietnam. It was so stained, cloudy and scarred that light wouldn't pass through it. Yet it was treated like the Holy Grail. This was a big-ticket item to the Carollas. It was considered a durable good in our household—on par with an automobile or a washing machine.

This grizzled container was probably as old as me when we reached peak cheapness. I was around twenty-five, and was a struggling starving-artist–bachelor barely staying afloat doing construction. I would go over to my grandparents' house for Sunday dinner, when my Hungarian step-grandfather would make a giant kettle of goulash. There'd always be plenty left over and I'd get to take some home. On more than one occasion, he would be ladling the stew into the solitary piece of Tupperware in my grandmother's house and I would hear, from my seat in the other room, her come into the kitchen and hit him with some stern words. "What are you doing? No! Give him the mayonnaise jar."

My grandmother felt I could not be trusted with the sacred Tupperware. She acted as though it had come over on the *Mayflower* and been passed down generation to generation. I lived three blocks from them, was their flesh and blood and had no history of theft and yet my grandmother forced my grandfather to take the goulash out of the Tupperware and put it into the Best Foods mayonnaise jar with the rusty, crusty metal lid.

I don't know what she thought would happen. Did she imagine that as soon as the Tupperware and I got out of the house I'd dive into my mini-pickup truck and head to Mexico to start a new life? I was broke as shit. I was definitely going to come back the next Sunday to refill said Tupperware with more goulash.

This is just one of a million examples of the poverty mentality that permeated my family. I've declared that I will never force my kids to endure these feelings. I suggest that you do the same. Because the real message you send when you act like a cheap bastard is not "take care of your stuff." The message is "This item cost me over a dollar and it is not disposable. Our relationship, however, is."

We have a billion plastic snap-lid containers in our kitchen, and my kids can do whatever the fuck they want with them. I value my relationship with them more than a food-storage container. I can get a new one of those at the grocery store, I can't get a new son or daughter at the supermarket. At least, not without ending up in an Amber Alert situation.

 Speaking of those containers. Because I've got twins, I'm getting everything in the jumbo size now. I go to Costco and come home with a huge vat of mayonnaise and a kiddie pool of peanut butter. And then I get into that argument with the wife when we're scraping the bottom of the container but it's still taking up a beer keg worth of room in the fridge. "There's still enough in there for one sandwich." "It's empty." "You have to scrape the bottom of it." I hate the space it takes up, but I can't bring myself to just chuck it out like Lynette would.

So here's my solution. Why not equip every jumbo-sized container of mustard or barbecue sauce with a little escape pod on the side, like the dock of the International Space Station? Just a small container that holds two ounces on the side, so when you're done with the five-gallon bucket of Dijonnaise, you can scrape the remnants at the bottom into the little bladder on the side, twist it, snap it off, put a cap on it and put it back in the fridge. That way you've got just enough for one more sandwich, and will have reclaimed the space above the crisper. Coming soon to a store near you: The Ace Carolla Condiment Dinghy.

2. EVEN IF YOU'RE NOT INTERESTED, FAKE IT . . .

Both historically and currently, my parents haven't been able to give a shit about shit I give a shit about.

My father would read a book in his living room every Friday night. Ironically, the light by which he was reading was partly supplied by the lights from the North Hollywood High football stadium where I was playing. He never worked on Friday nights, he just preferred to stay home and read Leo Buscaglia rather than see me play for the North Hollywood High Huskies. He wasn't interested in football and that was that.

This is a trend that continues today.

Last year, my dad called to say he wanted to come over and see the twins. I told him they were out on one of their many activities; I believe it was seeing the Harlem Globetrotters. I started going into how the kids were constantly jet-setting and doing amazing stuff. As an example, I casually mentioned, "I just did the voice in a big Disney movie, so they were walking the red carpet last night." I waited a moment for him to ask the name of the movie, and what my part in it was. Never happened. He just moved on. That, or he thought I was lying.

It's not like Dad hates the stuff that I do. It's just not on his radar. He's not the Great Santini, he's the Great Doesn't-Give-A-Shit. For the entire time I have been doing my home-improvement podcast *Ace on the House* he's called it *Ace on the Roof*. And on the very first morning of my radio show after I took over from Howard Stern, I famously gave him a ten-thousand-dollar challenge. There were five questions of Adam Carolla trivia. I told my dad that if he got the first one right, he'd walk away with ten grand. My very own ten grand. It wasn't money the station had put up, and we didn't have a sponsor. I had my checkbook next to me as I gave him the questions. I was that confident in his impending failure. With each question, the payday would be cut in half. So if he screwed the pooch on the first one he still had a chance at five thousand, then twenty-five hundred, and so on.

Now, bear in mind, this is my father. His best financial year ever was about forty-seven thousand dollars. He now had a chance to make more in one minute than in two months of the best year of his life, and all he had to do was provide some well-known facts about his own son.

Here was the first question, for ten thousand: "Your son was on a legendary radio station for the past ten years. Name that radio station's call letters and number."

As the drum roll rolled, he stammered out an answer. He knew it was K-rock but couldn't spell it: KROQ. He went with KROC.

I decided to be merciful, and see if he could pull out the number, 106.7. He said 950. Jimmy, who was in the studio that day and sitting next to him, noted he didn't even have the right frequency.

Then, for five thousand, I asked, "I did a television show on a popular cable network that had to do with puppets making phone calls. The name of that show was . . ." After a good minute of his hemming and hawing, I pulled the plug. I told him it was called *Crank Yankers* and then noted that Jimmy, again sitting nineteen inches from him, was wearing a *Crank Yankers* T-shirt. I was stunned on the third question when he *was* able to pull out my *Loveline* partner's last name: Pinsky. Now, before you give him too much credit, Dr. Drew had recently given him a referral to a urologist and he needed Drew's full name when he filled out the forms.

Credit where credit is due, my dad recently came over to see the kids and I had him watch the documentary I made on Paul Newman's racing career. I was floored when he not only liked it, but said, "If you never do another thing, that will be enough." I was astonished. I've never gotten a reaction from him like that on anything I've ever done. It felt like an *Invasion of the Body Snatchers* moment. He could have come out of the closet and broken cover as the world's top gay CIA agent and it would have been more credible to me.

But the Lord giveth and the Lord taketh away. When I showed the same film to my mother, she piped up with, "I'm not interested in the subject matter, but it held my interest." I loved the documentary *King of Kong*. I'm not into arcade games but I enjoyed it. That's the point of a documentary; it's supposed to capture your interest in something you know nothing about. But that's about as much of a compliment as she was capable of. She gave me what the great Albert Brooks, when doing my podcast, called "the complisult": a compliment couched in an insult.

The saddest part is that in my mom's mind, this *was* a compliment. But the message conveyed is that the thing I cared enough about to make a documentary about she was not interested in. The thing your son is passionate about is of no interest to you. Maybe I should do my next documentary on her, because I find her lack of interest in my interests very interesting.

Ultimately the lesson is this: whether it's their finger painting when they're three or their salesman-of-the-month award when they're forty-three, you have to put in some telenovela-quality acting to pretend you give a shit. Because you do. Maybe not in your kids' hobbies or minor accomplishments. No, the thing you give a shit about, or should, is your relationship with them.

3. DON'T BE A BUMMER

My parents were both total downers. My mom was a hippie who, ironically, had friends named Sunshine and Happy, but was a dark cloud and never mustered a smile. There was a constant bad vibe in my house growing up. I was inundated with messages about the indigenous people and how we were oppressing them, how horrible white people were, how it was all going to end in a nuclear holocaust anyway. These were great motivators for getting your kid up and ready for school. "Sure, son, you can go to school but it doesn't matter. Khrushchev is going to nuke us all anyway." You probably think I'm joking, unless you grew up in the sixties. Two of the most popular songs at the time were "Where Have All the Flowers Gone" by Peter, Paul and Mary, and "Eve of Destruction" by Barry McGuire. Here are a couple of lines from the McGuire tune.

> If the button is pushed, there's no runnin' away
> There'll be no one to save with the world in a grave

This isn't coming from some unknown singer/songwriter at a coffeehouse. This was a *Billboard* number-one song the year after I was born. This is what I grew up with. My parents lapped this shit up.

When I was somewhere in single digits my mom read one of those 1970s parenting books about how not to fuck up your kid. She must have fallen asleep before the end. I guess there weren't enough pictures. When you're reading one of these books, it's already too late. The damage is done. Somewhere in the book it told her not to say, "I don't like you," but rather, "I don't like what you do." So at one point she used that line on me and I fired back instantly with, "I am what I do." I must have been seven at the time, but I already knew that she was feeding me a bunch of hippie nonsense.

This is the same "love the sinner, hate the sin" mind-set that Christian conservatives have about the gays. Something I'm sure my uber-liberal mother would be completely against. Moreover, if on that day in the early nineteen seventies I had asked her to separate Nixon or Henry Kissinger from their actions and see them as people, she would have given me a dozen reasons why the logic she had just spat out didn't apply in those cases.

So I bring the opposite of this message to my parenting. My kids are their actions. I'm never going to pull that "no matter what you do, I love you" bullshit. If Sonny decides to shoot up his college I'm not going to think, "Well, he's still my son . . ." By that logic, we all could have been friends with Hitler. "Adolf, I love you man. But I don't like what you do. The whole ethnic cleansing holocaust thing I don't like. But you, as a person and a painter. Terrific."

Among the other hippie bullshit my mom adhered to was her biorhythm wheel. For those of you who've never heard of this (and congratulations on that, you were raised by sane people) it's supposedly calibrated to your birthday to tell you what your biorhythms are and whether you're going to have a good day. There'd be something called an "extra critical" day when you were in transition from one phase to another during which it was not a good idea to operate a motor vehicle, leave the house or do anything really. At least, that's how my mom used it. To her, every day was an extra critical day. Or so it seemed. Any time I needed her to do anything, like give me a ride to Teddy Lewis's house three miles away in Van Nuys, it seemed to be an extra critical day and she needed to continue vegetating in our Valley shitbox. She actually had a twenty-four-hour-notice policy for getting a ride so she could consult the biorhythm wheel. I kid you not.

This thing that ruled my mom's life when I was a kid was about as scientific as a mood ring. But it allowed her to validate the lazy, downtrodden, checked out, scared-of-life lifestyle she had come to know and love, and thus make no attempt to change it. It was as if for every decision she consulted a Magic Eight Ball with only one fortune, reading, "Fuck Off."

So growing up in this depressing soup definitely damaged me. And I won't do that to my kids. My mom is still living this way. I've always said that she has three modes: "has a cold," "just getting over a cold," or "feels something coming on." This is a great way to get out of stuff. Once people learn you're that person, they stop expecting anything. No matter what, I will be there for my kids. Plus I never get colds because I'm not one of those anti-vaccinating, Purell-soaked cowards.

My mother is incapable of admitting or acknowledging happiness. I once bet my buddy Ray that if he called her and she said she was doing "good," instead of "okay" or "fine," I would give him a thousand dollars. There was a risk. Ray doesn't call my mom often, so if he rang she might put on a brave face and lie. But I felt confident. He called her up and asked how she was doing. Her immediate answer was "not so good." I never even needed to take my wallet out.

Here's another move my mom had, and still has, that I will never pull on my kids. Whenever you ask her anything, there is a slow, long exhale before she answers. You could ask her something simple like what time it was and when she was finished deflating herself it would be a full minute later than when you asked. Every question is met with a tired-of-life sigh as if to say, "I wish this breath were my last."

I would rather have been physically abused than lived with the total zeros that my parents were. My house was as lively as a funeral at a methadone clinic.

4. HAVE A PASSION

On that note, one thing I do opposite from my dad is have passion. If you asked my dad for his favorite team or performer, he'd not be able to provide it. He has zero passion for anything. He likes jazz and, if you really pressed him, he might say he's a fan of Tony Bennett or Dave Brubeck, but he doesn't have all their records, or autographs or books about them. This is something I cannot understand, and I vow I will not pass on this level of indifference to my kids.

That sends two incredibly negative messages. First, that life is not to be embraced fully and deeply, that it can be squandered. My father lived his life like he was going to live to be eight thousand years old. He didn't throw himself into anything, the way that I, an atheist who believes you only get one go 'round and that the clock is ticking, does. Second is about identity. I'm "a car guy" and "a comedian" and "a builder." I could add another twenty to that list. My dad was " ." He later became "a therapist," but when I was growing up, he was blank space. It's very unsettling for any kid to have a parent who, as far as engagement with life, isn't really there. It's like being raised by a vending machine. You could get from it the minimum suste-

Sonny always sees me get excited about my vintage-car races. I think that's good. I think as much as you need to participate in whatever your kid is into, they need to see and occasionally participate in what you, the parent, are passionate about. It sends the right message. We're constantly wringing our hands about tutors and discipline and nutrition. One of the most important things you can show your kids is that you care about something. Show them things that are important are worth the effort: building a business, preparing a car for a race, improving your home, whatever you're passionate about.

But don't go overboard. You don't want your kids to be like those preachers' kids who get beaten, literally and figuratively, with the Bible. When you make everything a sin, you're asking for trouble because eventually the kid is going to get a boner, decide that means he's evil, say "fuck it," and go get into some disgusting porn. Rebellion is the nature of teens. Well, I rebelled against my parents' lethargy, so I hopped in a vintage race car and hit the track. If my dad had been into vintage racing maybe I'd be at home doing the crossword puzzle instead. So show them you care about something, about living, but don't demand that they also get into that particular thing, too. On that note . . .

5. IT'S NOT ABOUT YOU

The most important lesson I learned from Jim and Kris Carolla, a lesson I choose to ignore, was how to be selfish parents.

I'll give them credit, they didn't cram their interests down my throat. But a lot of that has to do with, as mentioned, not having any. My parents were the opposite of those Dance Moms who force their kids into pageants under the guise of "This is her dream; she wants to do it." Bullshit. It's clearly about your unfulfilled dreams. I hate those nut jobs talking about their pageant kids saying, "They've wanted to do it ever since they were three." Three-year-olds have no control over their lives. If you don't want your kids competing in pageants, you hold the power, not them. I sincerely doubt a six-year-old would hitchhike to the banquet room at the Sheraton and compete in the Little Miss Shaker Heights pageant herself if her emotionally damaged Mommy wasn't pushing her.

But my folks, without fail, make it about themselves. Always have, always will. For example, in 2011, shortly after my first book came out, I was adapting some of the material from the book into a live stand-up show at the El Portal Theater in North Hollywood (interestingly enough, a former movie theater I had been to several times as a kid) and needed some visuals. I called my mom to see if she had some old family photos that I could use to illustrate some stories. She replied with, "There might be a shoebox in the closet." A few days later, on the day of the show, I called to see if I could swing by and grab them.

Now, I've learned over the years not to ask my mom for anything. Or my dad, for that matter. Their M.O. is to be wildly ineffective and difficult, so everyone learns not to bother them. It's like announcing you have a bad back. No one asks you to help them move when you pull that trick.

I didn't think this was a big ask. My mom lived in nine hundred square feet, and finding that shoebox full of old pictures shouldn't have been too much trouble.

When I called that day, I was hoping she had found the energy to help me out. "Can I swing by and grab that box and go through it?" She replied, "Me and your stepfather are making health drinks right now, I don't really have the time. Could you come by in a few hours, like around two?" This was about eleven in the morning on a Saturday. The show was that night and I was behind. I said, "I have to go to North Hollywood to take a bunch of pictures, then up to La Crescenta to take a picture of that old house, too. The show is tonight. I'm really up against it and swamped. I could be there in the next half hour. Just get it from the closet, I'll come in and grab it and be out of your way." She, after a long sigh, said, "I don't know . . ." So I threw in a sarcastic, "Forget it. Enjoy your health drink." With no awareness at all, she then asked for four free tickets to the show that she put zero effort into helping me prepare. Think about the symbolism of that. Message received, Mom, you're taking care of you. I said a very sarcastic, "Thanks a lot. I appreciate all the help. I'll get your four tickets," and hung up.

And that's the lesson for all you parents reading this. If you're reading this book while your kid is on the field playing football, put it down and watch them play. Being a parent is about putting your shit on hold. You'd like to buy a recliner; instead, you're buying car seats. You'd like to drive a two-door convertible; instead you're driving a minivan. You'd like to take a Hawaiian vacation; instead, you're saving it for private school. There's a monetary sacrifice, but there's also a personal one. You'd like to just plop down in front of the television when you get home exhausted, but your kids want to see you, so you better get down on the floor and build that Lego castle. The more you're into you, the worse the parent you are. We always think about the parents who are physically violent or alcoholic. You show me someone who is narcissistic and self-absorbed, and I'll show you a miserable kid. That's why no one should have kids at seventeen. You don't give a shit about anybody but yourself at that age. And for the next eighteen years of that kid's life, you're going to have to do a lot of shit you don't want to do. That's what being a parent is. You'll want to see *No Country for Old Men* but instead you're going to *A Dolphin Tale 2*. And guess who ends up paying.

But, you know what, it's worth it. You might be miserable spending time and money on shit you don't want to do but in the end it buys you something more valuable, a relationship with your kids. When you don't show an interest in their interests, can't feel or at least feign joy when you're around them, when you make life with them seem like a chore, you pretty much guarantee that they'll resent you. And, if you're really unlucky, you run the risk of them writing their fourth book containing tales of your half- and, occasionally, quarter-assed parenting. I guess Sonny and Natalia should be grateful their paternal grandparents were such turds. Without them, I'd have a lot less vitriol to power my podcast and thus fill the family coffers. And I wouldn't have such a clear roadmap of what *not* to do as a parent. And I pass that roadmap on to you, dear readers. Let my pain be your gain.

CHAPTER 8

☞ To Sonny and Natalia, on Buying Your First House

HERE'S SOME ADVICE for my kids that I think all of you parents can give your own children on the other big purchase of their lives: their first house. If you don't think that buying a house is the greatest symbol of achieving the American dream, then put down this book and move to Russia.

Dear Sonny and Natalia,

One thing that I have attempted to beat into you, and I hope I was successful, is that you should be owners, not renters. Owning a home is a good investment, there are tax benefits, it will fill you with pride, it will force you to become handy and make you get your financial shit together. And you won't have to deal with douchebag landlords.

But here's a fair warning. Owning a house will turn you into an asshole. Your mother says that's when I became one. Pretty much since the day we met, we have had a constant running dialogue about me being an asshole, but when you were eight we finally nailed down the point of no return, the moment when I made the final conversion to full assholedom. She said it was when I was thirty-four, and I bought my first house.

Nine out of ten asshole-ish behaviors are connected to your home. You have to yell at the gardener for leaving the pool gate open for the thousandth time, you have to yell at your kids for scratching up the hardwood floor and you have to scream at your wife, "I'm asking you to *call* the carpet guy, not clean the carpet yourself!" I think when you sign the deed to your house, the realtor should present you with the keys, and a brown blazer with a toilet paper roll embroidered on the lapel and say "Congratulations, you're now officially an asshole."

When you're renting, you don't give a shit about your domicile. It's temporary. If your friend drops a bowl of salsa on the carpet you're pissed, but not irate. You know that eventually you'll just move out and move on to another rental. When it's your home, that means you own said carpet and can do math on how much you paid for it and how many more hours you're going to need to work to replace it. So, Sonny and Natalia, get ready to become assholes just like your old man.

But I'd rather you be assholes than losers. The renters reading this are now pissed, but please, take it as motivation and coming from one who knows of the loserdom whence he speaks. My history with home-owning and shitty apartments is well detailed in my second book, so check it out if you haven't, and you'll see that I speak purely out of experience and concern. I was pathetic back when I rented. Here's a great way to tell if you're a loser who needs to step it up in the life department and get yourself into a home of your own: When you are asked to house-sit for a friend who does have their shit together are you excited? Can you not wait to get out of your squalid shitbox? Do you want to squat in that home and change the locks so that your friend can't ever get in again? Then you're a loser, and need to figure it out.

I used to be that guy. I house-sat for a friend once and was far too excited. It was a two-bedroom with no pool in a dumpy part of Los Angeles, Van Nuys to be exact, but it was far superior to the crappy apartment I was renting with a couple of other losers. When that house-sitting run was done, I was deflated to go back to my apartment.

Between the time you were born and when I'm writing this, we moved. Frankly, I wouldn't be surprised if, by the time you read this, we will have moved again. Anyway, a few years after you came along, we moved from the hills of Hollywood to La Cañada. Your mother and I decided that, among many other reasons to get outside of Los Angeles proper, we wanted you to have a place to ride bikes and a real backyard to do cartwheels and throw a football around in. That place was great. But, less than ten months after we moved there, into this great house with a tire swing and zip line, Natalia, you announced that you wanted to step it up and live in a place like Uncle Jimmy. So forgive me if I assume by the time you're reading this letter that we've moved one or two more times due to your unreasonable demands.

By the way, moving a lot as a kid is another in my long line of rich man, poor man examples: things the very rich and the very poor have in common that people in the middle class don't share. When you're super rich you move a lot, constantly stepping it up or moving when business requires. When you're super poor you're constantly on the lam or getting evicted. The middle class just buy a two-bedroom, ranch-style house in the burbs and wait to die in it.

Closely connected to that is living in the same house as your grandparents. (Though credit where it's due, one of my listeners came up with this one.) The really rich live in the manor that has been in their family since the Civil War, and the really poor are sharing a doublewide with Granny, Mama, Mama's third boyfriend in as many months and their six brothers and sisters.

So, with all of this in mind, what should you be looking for in your first, and hopefully last, house?

Space: Famous racecar driver/builder Carroll Shelby once said that, when it comes to winning races, there's no substitute for cubic inches. And not-so-famous driver/builder, me, once said when it comes to relationships there is no substitute for square footage. When you and your spouse are literally up each other's ass because you don't have a big enough place, it's going to cause marital strife. The bright side of this is that when you inevitably get divorced you won't have much property to fight over.

Trust me. A guy could move into a studio apartment with a Victoria's Secret model and within two days he'd be ready to shiv her with a sharpened toothbrush.

The bottom line is that you can live in a three bedroom for nine years or a one bedroom for nine months. Also, more square feet usually means more than one television, and separate TiVos. There's no sense in getting in a fight with your old lady because *Top Gear* and *Top Chef* come on at the same time.

A Nice Yard: A house is more than just the four walls you sleep in. You need that yard to throw a baseball, chase the dog around and, this one is directed at you, Sonny, take a piss in.

Yes, Natalia (and all you other ladies reading this), you'll never quite understand what a power move this is. Taking a piss in your own yard feels so liberating. Being a dude has its cons for sure, like dying several years earlier, but a big pro is that you can literally pee anywhere. Imagine you've been driving home with a bladder full of piss. Instead of having to fumble with your keys, unlock the door and race up to the bathroom, you can just step out of your car, unzip and water the bushes. Because those bushes are yours. If you did this in your apartment complex you'd be arrested, and if you did it on someone else's lawn, they'd shoot you with rock salt. This is the patch of ground that God created and that you worked hard to own, and no one can stop you from putting your urine in it. Go for it. Plus, that stuff has a smell and it might ward off some predators.

And on that note, Sonny, I'm guessing you'll be about my height, so when you buy that first house, make sure the bathroom sink is at optimal piss height, too.

A Cul-De-Sac: If you can manage it, you want to live on a cul-de-sac. That way you don't have assholes like me zooming up and down your street plowing into my future grandkids on their hoverboards. And make sure it's *called* a cul-de-sac. There is a big difference between a cul-de-sac and a dead end. They're both streets that have no outlet but at the end of one is a back entrance to a golf course, and at the end of the other is a couch with raccoons fucking on it.

Basement: This might be a tough one to pull off if you stay in Southern California, or the Southwest in general. For some reason there are no basements out here. Basements are great. It's like adding a second or third story to your house. And it's always fifteen degrees cooler down there.

I'm thinking about this more for my future grandson. Without a basement, where is he supposed to lose his virginity? Every kid from the East Coast or the Midwest lost their virginity in a basement. Growing up in SoCal, we had to go out and hump in a car. If you had a compact car, it sucked. Getting it on in the back of an '82 Honda Civic could literally cramp your style.

Plus, there's just something truly great about going down those creaky wooden stairs to a basement workshop and refinishing an old coffee table, playing a few games of darts or grabbing a Sawzall and dismantling a hooker corpse. Perhaps I've said too much.

Bar-Free Windows: Windows with bars are something you want to avoid, and an immediate sign that you should move on with your house search. This may not resonate with people outside of Los Angeles, but almost all the houses here have bars on first-floor windows. That's how much this town sucks.

Here's how you know you're in a horrible neighborhood: There are bars on the windows of the houses, but the bars in the neighborhood have no windows. Heavy.

So You've Found Your Dream Home

Make sure you get a home inspection before you close. Just understand that there's going to be shit to fix. Every home is a fixer-upper. Don't walk away from a good place because you don't like the paint job or a few windows are drafty. There's always something to do, and you should appreciate that. Make the home yours. But here's a bit of paranoia you can just ignore, and that is mold inspections. I don't think humans would exist if mold could really kill us. We currently have a very bizarre relationship with mold. We devour blue cheese and penicillin, but will freak out if we find it during a home inspection. This is just white people panicking over nothing. Ironically, you never hear about black mold affecting black people. It's always the wealthy white folk who also coincidentally have allergies to lactose, gluten and life.

Okay, so you've found your dream house; now it's time to purchase it. Just like your first car, don't come crawling to me. You're going to have to earn it just like I did. I didn't ask your grandfather to take out a second mortgage on his piece of shit in the Valley to help me out. Not that he would have, anyway. So unless you've married a rich guy or carved out a nice career in gay porn (that goes for either of you), you're going to need a loan.

Here's what you need to know about the mortgage process. There is no such thing as good credit. There's only bad credit and not bad

credit. Every real-estate transaction I've ever made required me to sign a Library of Congress's worth of paper and go through FBI level interrogations. I've done several sizeable real-estate deals and every time it's the same. I've never defaulted on a loan; I've never been foreclosed on. I should have the kind of credit where I can walk into any person's home and say, "This is my house now, get out." But I'm still treated like a guy who operates a forklift and is trying to buy his first one-bedroom town house.

Moving In and Moving On
So you've secured your home, signed the deed and changed the locks. Now it's time to move. Here's a few things that you should be aware of.

First, don't do this yourself. That couple of hundred bucks you shell out on movers will be the best money you ever spend. Not only are you saving your back, you're saving your friendships because without hiring movers you're going to rope your poor buddies into doing it and they're going to resent you later. You're essentially saying, "Here's a job that I'd pay a stranger five hundred bucks to do, but since we're so close I'll give you a six-pack of Heineken." And you can almost guarantee that it will be a friend who accidentally drops the heirloom china or breaks your framed autographed picture of Mr. T. You'll never see the mover again, but it's going to be awkward hanging with your friend who tripped and dumped Nana's urn on the lawn.

So hire movers, and then lower your expectations. Something is going to get scratched or broken. It's just part of the process. Don't be an asshole to the poor bastard who's wearing the back support just trying to make a few bucks moving your fridge.

In fact, here's another tip: Tip. Moving is so expensive that people usually just pay the fee, call it a day and then complain when the dresser gets scratched. They never think to add a gratuity for the guys literally doing the heavy lifting. So tip the guys in advance and maybe they'll take a little extra care. They're used to getting nothing but attitude at the end of the move when they're covered in sweat and dreaming of a cold beer and Vicodin. They'll appreciate the extra cash, trust me.

Make sure you give the tip out when all the movers are together. I've noticed in all of my moves that there is always an alpha mover. He's usually the older of the two guys, the cagey veteran of the moving van. If you tip that guy when he's alone, you know he's just stuffing it in his pocket and stiffing the poor college student working at the moving company on weekends. Make sure the wealth gets spread around and gets in their hands in advance, so they'll put in a little extra hustle and not put an end to your end table.

You might not have room for all your stuff in your new place. Even if you move it on up to a bigger abode, sometimes the furniture you had in one place just doesn't fit into the new one. Or the new house already has a fridge and you no longer need the old one. And in general it's good to get rid of stuff before you move, so there's less to pack and break the movers' backs. So instead of hanging on to stuff you don't really need or use, just dump it. Don't do the storage unit thing. The Carollas are a long line of hoarders (except we didn't really have anything to hoard). Don't fall into this trap. You'll be happier if you just leave that old stuff behind, and replace it if you need to. It makes no sense to go out and get a storage unit just in case you want that bread maker in three years. If you haven't used it in a year, donate it, have a yard sale or use it for target practice.

Those storage-unit commercials paint a much sunnier picture of themselves than is accurate. The roller door slides up to reveal the storage-unit renters and they're delighted. It's always happy families going to their clean storage unit to get out the water skis.

Bullshit. Everyone is miserable at those places. It means your abode is smaller than you like, and you can't even find nine-by-nine to keep a bunch of stuff you don't need but are too pathetic to part with. Or your old lady kicked you out, you're crashing on a buddy's couch and you put all of your shit in storage until you get your own pad. In L.A., those places are all under freeway overpasses, the sun hasn't shined on them in decades and the only people who are more miserable than the people who go there are the people who work there. If you have to put "do not attempt" on car commercials where the SUV is doing some off-roading, these storage-unit company ads should have a disclaimer, too. "Warning: Professional Actors Portraying Gross Exaggeration of Happiness."

The last one I saw featured a mother showing her daughter her wedding dress. Mom is taking her dress out of the box and the girl is over the moon. Awesome. She gets to wear Mama's mothbally, was-white-but-is-now-yellow wedding dress covered in a Rorschach test of semen stains. In storage-unit history, has there ever been a mother presenting her daughter with her thirty-five-year-old wedding dress to her delight? Has that ever happened? I say nay. Could you imagine saying to your twenty-two-year-old daughter, "We're going out wedding dress shopping." "Where, Beverly Hills?" "No, we're heading to the storage unit under the 110 Freeway." She'd beat her mom with the table lamp she also kept in the storage unit.

Home Alone?

One of the things you'll find out quickly when you own your home is that even if you're single, you're not there alone. There are ants, spiders, cockroaches, rats, bats, snakes and various other creatures taking up residence in your residence. Sorry, Sonny, but this is one gender role that is still intact. You, as a male, will be the exterminator in your home, unless you end up gay, and then you two can flip for it. Either way, here are a few tales and tips.

Spiders: These little bitches seem to be out of control. Every house has spiders, but the ones we have in our house as I'm writing this seem to be some turbo-charged, over-caffeinated breed. They'll get a web up while you blink and it's not cute, symmetrical *Charlotte's Web* stuff, it's like something MC Escher would shoot out of his ass. It looks like Johnny Depp took his multiple scarves off and threw them in a ball on the chair.

I walked into my bathroom at four in the morning, and there was a giant spider on the wall. I felt like the stepparent who came home early and found the teen banging away at his girlfriend on the couch. I was thinking, is this what goes on all the time when I'm asleep? The spider noticed me and froze. He was probably like, "What are you doing up at this hour, old man? Time to get that prostate checked." Then, he scurried behind a mirror. It was a stalemate. I couldn't go back to bed knowing it was there, but the mirror was too heavy to move. I ended up blowing into the crack behind the mirror to try and coax the thing out the other side so that I could smash it. I endured an hour-long retarded Mexican stand-off with an arachnid, instead of catching the zzzzs I need to be able to work and thus afford to house that spider. And my kids.

They always make their appearance at the worst time. Once, about two years ago, I was all set to crash after a long day. I had done a couple of gigs that afternoon, came home, had a couple of Mangrias and headed off to bed. When I flipped on the light, there was a spider hanging out on the ceiling. I was a little wobbly from the day and the Mangria, and standing on a pillow-top mattress, so it was tough to get that little fucker with the toilet paper. You also have to be sure to pick the right amount of toilet paper. Too little, and you can feel the thing crunch, which you don't want. It's just gross and its guts will leak through the TP and onto your hand. But, if you use too much, it will create a soft nest for the thing, and it will just scurry away to fight another day. This particular day I didn't have my TP ratio right, because I ended up with two spider legs in the paper, and the now wounded and angry spider was nowhere to be found. It landed somewhere in the bed and I just knew it was biding time until my head hit the pillow to come back and take up residence in my ear hair.

Rats: You'll eventually get one of these lovely vermin in your house, too. No matter how manly you think you are, Sonny, when you see that little rat tail scurrying, you will turn into a 1950s cartoon housewife. You'll be up on a footstool on your tippy-toes, freaking out. I don't know why rats scare us so much, but they do.

It would be weird to explain our relationship with rats to an alien. They give us our greatest scientific advances, but if we see them in our kitchen at night, we go after them with a tennis racquet. Apparently, we share many biological attributes with rats, but we still want to kill them. We don't have that range of emotions with dolphins, for instance. It might be a grudge because rats spread the plague. Plus, in the '80s, there were all those vans painted with evil renditions of rats with fangs cheating at cards. Rats get a bad rap. They're not looking for trouble and when you turn on the light they run away. It's not like you come home and a rat is banging your girlfriend. I think the real problem is their posture. Rats always look like they're up to no good. In Disney movies, the hero always has great posture and the villain is always hunched over. Hummingbirds have great posture and we love them. But the rat is our mortal enemy. We'd all probably have rats as pets if they would just hit the chiropractor and take care of that scoliosis.

Snakes: You kids already know that where we live we have rattlesnakes. You may have been too young to remember when our dog, Molly, was bitten by a rattler. A year or so later, our gardener found a rattlesnake as he was making his appointed rounds with the hedge clippers. Because of those two incidents, your mom decided that not only did we need to get Molly rattlesnake-aversion–trained, but we needed to have the snake wrangler come out and safety proof the place for you two.

First off, I'm not even sure if what the gardener found was an actual rattlesnake. There are nonpoisonous snakes that look like rattlesnakes. They've taken on that camouflage, so birds of prey and coyotes won't go at them. What the snakes didn't factor in when evolving that camouflage was the fireman who gets called out by Lynette to chop them in half with a flathead shovel.

So, anyway, despite me and my wallet's protest, the snake-proofing guy came and laid down a powder that smelled like mothballs and tampons put in a Cuisinart (by the way, Mothballs and Tampons is my favorite morning zoo team). He sprinkled this powder in a big circle around the perimeter of the house. This all seemed like a good plan until my assistant, Jay, piped up with, "What if there are snakes that are already under the house? Doesn't that just keep them in?" Thanks, Jay, for working the wife up all over again. You're fired.

Flies: Every house has flies. That's just inevitable. They're called house flies for a reason. Amazingly, we're well into the 2000s as I write this, and we still don't have a great way to kill them. Inevitably, you'll get that fly buzzing around and go looking for a flyswatter and not be able to find it. It's a twenty-nine-cent item, but you'll only buy one and thus spend an hour looking for it. This very thing has happened to me. Just like everything I attempt to locate in my own home, someone had moved the flyswatter to some random drawer seemingly just to fuck with me.

Everyone thinks they're a ninja with the bar rag or T-shirt when it comes to flies, but you never manage to actually get the fly that way because the whoosh of air you create just pushes it to safety. And the catch-and-release plan never works either. It's nice to think that maybe that fly was a good person in a past life and you should give it its freedom, but it never pans out. I had a fly in the house once, and after chasing it around for an hour, I cornered it in the bathroom, then sucked in my stomach and slid out the crack in the door to give it a time out. But to the fly the bathroom is Valhalla, like a fat guy getting trapped in a Fogo de Chao. Eventually, I found the flyswatter and sent it to the big shit pile in heaven.

My point is that you're going to get these things a lot, so don't go for the fancy Sharper Image flyswatter that kills with electricity.

That shit never works. They're always trying to invent new fly-killing technology. This one uses lasers to shoot them down in midair, this one kills with telepathy; you put on a hat and think bad things about them. Just buy a half-dozen of those classic cheap plastic flyswatters and keep one in every room.

Must-Haves for Your First Abode

On that note, let me give you a list of other stuff you'll need to have in your home.

Blue LED Clock: This thing is a life changer. Totally worth the money. It sheds enough light so that you can find your way around at night. It doesn't need to play an iPod, it just needs to illuminate the room so that when you get up to take a piss you don't trip over the dog or have to turn the light on and wake up the wife or husband. It's not so bright it cuts through the eyelids, either. It's a nightlight for grown-ups, it keeps the room in a cool light and isn't shaped like Spiderman.

Dimmer Switches in the Bathroom: In that same vein, there's nothing worse than when you hit the bathroom in the middle of the night, turn on the light and have your eyeballs scream. That ends up waking you up completely, and you will struggle to get back to sleep. Or you piss in complete darkness and end up urinating into the potpourri dish, not noticing until someone decides to take a sniff and thinks, "I didn't know they made asparagus potpourri."

There's something about pissing in the dark that makes even the calmest among us freak out. Once when I brought Natalia over to Jimmy's for football Sunday, I took her for a piss in his first-floor bathroom. This is a small bathroom, with just a toilet and a sink. No windows. So when you shut the door there's no natural light (unless that's what you've been drinking). Well, after Natalia took her pee, Daddy decided to make a little water, too. And, as always, she decided to fuck with me. The light switch is inside the room and while I had my back turned out went the lights. While Natalia was laughing hysterically and I was yelling, "Turn the lights on," I noticed that I wasn't hearing the splashing of my tinkle hitting the toilet water. I started to panic and overcompensated trying to find it again. I ended up covering not just the floor and toilet in piss, but also a copy of Bill Simmons' book, *Basketball*, which was next to the toilet. Sorry, Bill. On the bright side, Jimmy definitely had to buy another copy.

Plus, when it comes to bathroom lights, you can never find the switch. There's no uniformity. Some bathrooms have the switch on the outside, some are on the inside, some are on the right side as soon as you enter the room and some are on the adjacent wall above the sink. So what you end up doing is feeling around in the dark like Helen Keller, running your hand over every crevice in the tile wall that is covered in years of fecal particulate. Can you think of anything other than the underside of the toilet seat that you less want to be running your hand over?

So when you have your own home you should install some dimmer switches with the little LED in them. (I love LED lights, in case you haven't noticed.) That way, you can find the toilet without pissing all over the place, and turning your shower into a golden shower, you don't shock your eyeballs with the overbright overhead light and you don't have to see how bad you look at four in the morning in your underpants.

Flashlights: I love me a good flashlight. It's something everyone needs, in every room of their home. You need one in each room because you never know where you'll be when the power goes out and you may just end up killing yourself on the stairs trying to find the flashlight in the dark.

That said, be careful what kind of flashlight you choose. Hopefully, the flaws with current flashlights will have been addressed by the time you're buying your first house.

Why do flashlights have to take fifteen different types of batteries, have fifteen different ways to turn them on, and have fifteen different settings? Can we get a little industry consistency? You know that setting where you can twist the front end and can illuminate an entire mountainside, or you can twist it tight the other direction and get a laser beam that will burn a hole in a piece of plate steel? Why? Shouldn't a flashlight just have a medium setting that we all agree on?

Then there are the ones that load the batteries from the front so that when you twist thinking you're making an adjustment, the top pops off and you dump them on the floor. Then there are the ones that take the batteries in the back but turn on by twisting the top. One takes four D cells, the other takes five C cells, another takes two AAs, while one is green and is powered by good vibes. Enough already.

Wouldn't we be living in a utopia if they were all just backloaders that took C cells, had an on/off button that was made of rubber and was red so it didn't blend in with the black of the goddamn flashlight? The bestselling flashlight in the world is a MagLight, which is traditionally black and has a little black rubber button. How the fuck are you supposed to see that at night when the power is out, which is the only time you'd ever be using it anyway? It's ironic that the device you need for light needs light to be activated. It might as well be solar powered.

Can you add a low-battery light, too? A little amber LED that tells you you're going to make it down the street to walk your dog but you're not going to make it back on those batteries. Everything else has a low battery warning—your phone, your smoke detector, your old lady's vibrator—why not your flashlight?

But again, they're cheap so just buy one for every room. Just don't buy black ones, for Christ's sake.

Disaster Kit: If you do decide to settle somewhere along the San Andreas Fault, you have to be prepared. I'm always surprised at how cavalier people are about disaster prep. I think it's our fear of death. We don't want to consider what we would do in case of an emergency. It's like picking out a gravestone. I would say that your average American has less than a day's worth of water set aside for a disaster. This is especially important here in California earthquake country, but every part of our nation is prone to some sort of disaster: hurricanes, tornados, blizzards, flash floods, race riots. You've got to get that disaster kit together. Tons of water, flashlights and batteries, crank-powered rechargeable radio so you can tune in for emergency messages, canned food and cash. Everyone forgets about cash. If the grid goes down, so do the ATMs.

You'll also need a generator. My agent James "Babydoll" Dixon was talking to me once about various home improvements he was making, and I suggested getting a generator. Not the cheap one with the ripcord to start it, I'm talking about a real one that's the size of a jukebox, that you pipe natural gas into and costs a couple of grand. You get an electrician to hook it up to the necessary circuits in your house: fridge, television, upstairs bedroom. You could even do one for the whole house, but that would be crazy expensive. I got into detail and told him exactly which one to get. A day or two after Hurricane Sandy hit New York in 2012, Babydoll managed to get to a computer and sent me an e-mail saying he wished he had listened to me when I told him to buy that generator. So be smart and listen to me now.

House Alarm System: I have mixed feelings on this whole issue. I think they are a good thing to have, and, of course, I want you guys to be safe, but I have not had great luck with these.

If I had to do it over again, I would do without a house alarm, even if it meant being bludgeoned in my sleep every four to six years. Alarm systems are so much hassle. There are always technical issues and almost daily dog-set-it-off situations. Life's too short, in my opinion.

At our prior abode, I had a bad sensor on a window that once made the alarm go off at three in the morning. The LAPD showed up at my house, shortly followed by TMZ. Enough said.

Also, let it be said that some of the diciest people you can let into your house are the guys who install home-security systems. These guys are losers who fell into that job. They didn't dream of this as kids and then go to Home-Security Installation College. These are guys who barely graduated high school and took the first gig they could to support their Oxycontin addiction. Ironically, the guy who installs alarms in your house generally has a longer rap sheet than the guy who might try breaking in.

The only ones who are worse are handymen and contractors. Trust me, I know.

Catching Contractors

Long before I was on the show *Catch a Contractor,* I knew that these guys were unethical dirtbags. Remember, I spent years working with, and for, them. No one gets into construction because they love drywall, it's because they hated school. If these guys could do anything else they would. Contractors live job-to-job, cutting as many corners as sheets of CDX ply, looking to stiff you at every turn. Every piece of lumber they rescue from a dumpster at another job site and then use at your house is one less that they then have to purchase and can thus convert into beer money.

Typically, contractors are three-time losers. A lot of them have sex offenses. They're not always full-on rapists but a lot of "I was twenty-seven and she was seventeen but she looked twenty" kind of stuff. And every one of them has at least one DUI. The second you leave these guys alone in your house, they can't decide whether to raid your pantry or sniff your panties.

So be cautious, get plenty of references, check their licenses online and check out their work in person when you are hiring a contractor. Never pay more than a 10 percent deposit to get started. Put together a payment schedule based on phases of the job: when rough plumbing and electrical are complete and the wall can be closed up, that's a draw. When the walls are closed and the nailing inspection on drywall is signed off by the inspector, that's another payment. And remember: change orders, change orders, change orders. This is documentation of an approved change to the original estimate. When you want something altered from the original bid, get it on paper. That's where shit always goes south.

And get multiple bids then take the one in the middle. The one that's too high means the guy is overcharging you; the one that's too low means he's cutting corners, is a hack who's in over his head and is going to screw you. The easy rule is to throw out the bid from the guy who pulls up in a tricked-out Humvee. If the next guy pulls up in a converted ice-cream truck with a lumber rack, you can toss that one, too. You're looking for a Ford F-150, three to seven years old, with a crew cab and cloth interior. Practical and durable, just like the job you expect him to do.

And do as much work as you can by yourself. (This goes for both of you. Don't underestimate yourself, Natalia. You might not do any framing or toilet installation, but you can certainly swap fixtures and pick up a paintbrush.) Not only will this help you avoid the scumbags that I used to work with, and am currently busting on *Catch a Contractor,* but it will instill in you the pride in ownership that's supposed to come with purchasing a house. It's yours, you worked hard to buy it, so take care of it yourself.

Home Improvement and Self-Improvement

When you have your own place I'd recommend that once a year you throw a party. It forces you to get your shit straight. Hoarders don't entertain. Your house is no different than your crotch. Let me explain. You show me someone's genitalia and I will tell you if they're single or have been in a loveless relationship for twenty-five years. They only clean up if they're getting laid. It's the same thing with a home. In both cases, if no one's coming over you're not trimming the bushes.

Having a party means that you give yourself a deadline to clean up, too. When we had your second birthday party we had it at a house I had bought as an investment property in Malibu. Now, since this wasn't where I was living day to day, the maintenance and home improvement would sometimes get away from me. I used your party as an excuse to kick my own ass into gear and finish it up. I still had people laying down sod during the party, literally. Guests were bumping into guys laying down turf and the paint was still drying. But we got the shit done.

You're probably going to be tempted, especially when you spend all your money on the down payment and moving expenses, to skimp on the décor and just make a run to IKEA. Please don't. IKEA is a human roach motel/ant farm. Once you're in, you can never get out. It's a giant maze that forces you to look at every single item. That's where they should have the L.A. marathon, because I've easily covered 26.2 miles walking around that place looking for a lampshade. You think you're going there for one thing and then you find yourself walking around for a full day holding a golf pencil.

I don't understand how that place operates. The profit margin eludes me. You can get fifteen hand-blown wine goblets for under two dollars. I understand when cheap crap comes from China but IKEA is based in Sweden. Isn't there some international law against using white people to make cheap shit?

And if you go there with your future husband or wife, be prepared to be going at each other with some forty-nine-cent steak knives before it's all over. One of you will stop to look at something and the other will keep walking, someone will get lost or forget to write down the number so you can find the dresser that you furiously negotiated over in the warehouse section later. Then you push the weird low-boy shopping cart to the register, send the other person to aisle 162 to get the particleboard coffee table and by the time they drag it back to you, you've already checked out or are holding up the line because getting to aisle 162 required crossing two time zones.

Then you'll send your spouse to get the car and back it into the loading zone. That's always a disaster because there are never enough spots, and by the time you get home to bust out the Allen wrenches, you're exhausted and on the verge of divorce.

I've done the IKEA run with your mother a couple of times. We have to do a whole war room thing before we head in. "I'm on Bravo team; you're Charlie company. Synchronize watches, we move in at 0200 hours and attack the kitchen section from the left flank." It never works. In the end I'm shopping for an entertainment unit and she's shopping for a divorce attorney.

Plus, even if you just ate at the Chili's across the parking lot before you walked in, you are still going to eat at IKEA. Two-point-seven hours of smelling Swedish meatballs will break down even

Michelle Obama. Swedish meatballs are underrated. They're savory. Savory's only competition is horny, as far as what it can get you to do. You cannot be around that smell and those visuals and not get some. The meatballs are cheap, too, like the furniture. It's like four bucks for a baker's dozen of delicious little balls. Swedish meatballs are the ukulele of food. They're the only thing that's better when smaller. You can't say that about tits.

No matter what project you're taking on, make sure to just get it done and over with. With home improvements you have to go start-to-finish with one vision. If you start a bathroom remodel and stop partway through, you'll never get to where you wanted to go. If you replace the sink one year, the mirror the next and the shower tile after that, nothing is going to match and your bathroom will look like a fucked-up patchwork mess.

If your home improvement projects get away from you, they will become part of your life. You'll be halfway through redoing your living room and the carpet will be rolled up in the corner. If you get distracted, six months will go by with the carpet roll taking up that space and it will just become like wallpaper, you won't even notice it anymore.

And on that note, let me close this letter with a wallpaper tale. I've always said that when picking wallpaper, just get three choices you feel good about, put them up on the wall, walk out of the room, walk back in, look at them for three seconds and pick one. You'll be at your purest at that moment. Listen to your gut.

Many years ago, your grandmother, my mom, was redoing her house, including the bathroom. And that bathroom, for a long time, was just bare drywall. She was in a one-bed, one-bath. It wasn't like this was the bath in the pool house or guest cottage. So one day I asked, "What's going on with the bathroom?" She replied, "What do you mean?" I said, "It's been like that for six months, when are you going to finish?" She said, "I'm picking out the wallpaper." I pointed out that the same four swatches were pinned to the wall for the past four months. She said, "I feel like you're judging me" and "I don't like your tone." I didn't have a tone. It was said very matter-of-factly. It was starting to get tense. I said, "I'm just trying to help; you've been looking at bare drywall for six months. You just have to trust your instincts and pick a swatch and go with it." Defensive, she said, "I don't like where this is going." So I shut up. And as I write this she's moving out of that house and into year three of redoing the piece of shit my grandmother lived in. It's a total lateral move from a one-bed, one-bath in the Valley to another. I haven't visited and I don't plan to. I'd definitely want to give home-improvement advice, something I'm literally an expert in. But I won't bother. I can't. It sends the wrong message. She got defensive for no reason and shut up the expert. This is like going to a doctor and telling him not to share his opinion. The scariest thing that can happen in a relationship is to have the other person not care. And that's what happened. She got me to not care. So whether it's home improvement, your career or how you dress, have an open mind and take people's commentary into consideration. The day people stop critiquing is the day that they stop caring.

So take all of that first-house advice and make use of it. And if by a miracle I'm still alive when you have your first home, remember, I criticize because I care.

CHAPTER 9

☞ To Sonny, on Puberty

Dear Sonny,

    As my work schedule will have likely killed me by the time you sprout your first pube, I'm not going to be around to have a man-to-man with you about becoming a man. This carries on a rich Carolla tradition of never having "the talk." It wasn't that my parents were uncomfortable about sex, it was that having "the talk" required talking.

A quick note to your sister: I'm very sorry, Natalia, you're just going to have to skip a few pages. I don't have any puberty advice for you. Talk to your mom about becoming a woman. I find periods confusing. I could never track when my girlfriends or wife had their period. They always seemed irritable. Maybe that just means I'm an asshole. But periods shouldn't even be called that, because they never seem to end. To me, periods seem like painting the Golden Gate Bridge. As soon as you're done, it's time to start over again.

I do have empathy for you. If I had a period once in my life I'd kill myself, never mind every month. I'd be the cuntiest of cunts if I had a period. I'm already constantly angry. If I had something coming out of me that I had to sop up with cotton, they'd have to lock me up like the Hulk or put me in chains like King Kong.

It's also a damn good thing that my friends and I don't have periods. Given the tea-bagging and other hazing that guys do to each other when they're adolescents, the potential for disgusting disaster would have been way up had periods been involved. There's no way that if my friend Ray had a bleeding vagina once a month, he wouldn't have put it on my face when I was sleeping.

Anyway, back to you, Sonny. You're going to have some hormonal shifts, too, just like your sister. Women will never appreciate the power of testosterone. When a boy hits puberty it's like Jesse Pinkman set up a meth lab in your nut sack. You'll have the uncontrollable urge to fight and fuck. You'll make stupid decisions without thinking. And you'll be angry. It's weird. There's a thing in life where up until your early twenties you're angry, then you mellow out a little bit, but then when you turn fifty-three you get angry again. On both ends of the spectrum, you don't give a shit and your anger makes you lash out. I call it the Alec Baldwin syndrome.

And of course this testosterone geyser is going to mean unintended and uncontrollable boners. Sorry, kid, this is just a storm you have to ride out. There's only a brief window in life where you have control over your junk. As a teen, you have zero control. You can be watching *Schindler's List* and get one. But when you're my age, chances are you'll be yelling at it to stand at attention. There's a sweet spot in your late twenties and early thirties when you no longer have to grab and tuck the surprise boner into your waistband to get rid of it because they don't happen so often. But right now, if you're reading this anywhere between the ages of fourteen and twenty-five, be prepared that a stiff breeze can give you a stiff dick.

Your entire body is going to go through some changes and with those body changes, come body issues. You're going to feel gangly and awkward. We have a national obsession with female body image. There's all those Dove soap love-your-body-type ads. And as a dad, even I have to admit it is fucked up what our culture foists on girls. I don't know if it's okay to masturbate to your kids' cartoons, but Disney princesses have no waists and giant boobs. The chick from *Aladdin* is crazy hot. What percentage of young girls watching those movies are gonna look like that? You would literally need your hips shaved off.

I feel bad for the girls, but what about the fellas? The Disney princes all have cleft chins, no waists and giant arms. There is no way that teenage boys can have that body without going on the juice. Every action figure is cut and has a hairless chest. If a girl aspires to look like a Disney princess or a Barbie doll all she needs to do is not eat. But boys need to get on HGH.

Women are always supposedly redefining beauty. They'll put Lena Dunham on the cover of a magazine and say she's brave and that she's redefining beauty. Well, for your sake, Sonny, in this book I'm redefining male beauty. Now men with a double chin and a hairy ass are beautiful. I have decreed it.

Speaking of hairy, with puberty comes hair in new and interesting places. So let's start at the head and work our way down, shall we?

Facial hair is a pain in the ass and I suggest you avoid it. If you got my genes you're not going to be able to grow a decent beard anyway. I have the beard of a black man: short, curly and itchy. I get ingrown hairs and the beard is always patchy.

Maintaining a beard is just a time suck unless you're a total dick like guys from the Jersey Shore who have to wake up at four in the morning to work their perfect sideburns. When you spend that much time working on your facial hair, you're just a narcissist who likes to spend a lot of time looking at yourself in the mirror.

At least go all or nothing. Either grow a full beard so you don't have to be bothered or shave every day or two and go clean. I've never understood the mustache. If you're going to spend the time scraping a blade across your face, just finish the job. And it's more than just the time. Dig this mustache thought.

Every other patch of hair on your body stinks: your armpits, your balls and your ass if you're me. Yet we cultivate the one right under our nostrils. Why would you want a stink sponge right under your nose? That would be like sewing your balls to your upper lip.

Please don't be that skinny young hipster guy with a beard. Beards are for guys that swing axes or play fiddles. Dan Hagerty or Charlie Daniels should have beards, not guys who punch up Adam Sandler scripts. A beard used to be something you earned. You were a lumberjack, a biker or a Civil War general. You haven't earned a beard at twenty-three.

We're currently in a facial hair free-for-all. We've gone through different phases throughout history, but now it's game on. It used to be that you had the same mustache or beard everyone else had. Now it's weird neck beards, or the Sharpie pinstripe, or the young guy with mountain-man beard right next to the guy with the waxed handlebar mustache. In the *Mad Men* era everyone was clean shaven and if they did want a mustache, they had one choice. Like all things for you kids nowadays, there's too much variety.

Just as the facial hair guy who loves to look in the mirror, the guy who has a very demanding and meticulous haircut is a narcissist, too. I was getting my hair cut recently, and the guy who was in the chair next to me when I sat down was still there giving instructions long after I was gone. I have no idea how long he was there before I sat down, but I paid the parking meter for thirty minutes and it had seventeen left when I got back behind the wheel. Meanwhile, this dude was still in the chair. He was a Russian guy getting some complicated two-stage fade haircut. Why? Because that's his one moment. His wife doesn't listen to him, his daughter hates his guts, his boss is up his ass and he has a job where he uses that tape-gun sealing boxes somewhere. This was his time to shine. This was his "me time." He's not in a barber's chair, he's on a throne and his lordship will have it his way. He's exerting his dominion over another person. It's wielding power. But how satisfying can that actually be?

Let's talk for a minute about the back of your hair. When you find a good barber shop (not a penny over twenty dollars, son), and it comes time for them to do the back of your neck they'll ask if you want it square or round. Just do what your old man does and say, "How did you do it last time? What is it now? Whatever it is, just do that." This whole conversation is a waste of time. Has anyone ever been passed over for a promotion, not gotten laid or gotten out of a moving violation because of what the back of their head looks like? I don't know what the back of my hair looks like as I write this book. I'm an adult, I'm married, and I know whatever shape it is in will just grow out anyway. So I don't give a fuck. My plan is, and yours should be, to spend as little time in that seat as possible. Every ten seconds extra I spend in the Model Cuts getting my thirteen-dollar haircut is ten seconds I could be making money and living my life. My hair is like the *Terminator,* it'll be back.

If you can get the straight razor shave at an upscale place like the Art of Shaving, go for it once in a while. It feels good. That hot lather, straight razor shave is nice, and makes you feel like Clint Eastwood in *The Outlaw Josie Wales* or an old-time gangster. You get out of there and want to hit a saloon and a whorehouse. That said, I can't sleep at night because the short leather strap used to sharpen the razor is called a strop. It looks like a strap and is shaped like a strap but for some reason is called a strop. This really bothers me for reasons that I cannot explain.

You're going to start getting hair on your chest, too. Just let it be. It's not even because the hair is difficult to tend to, it's that the chicks who are attracted to the guys with shaved chests are the chicks who are attracted to *all* guys with shaved chests and therefore you're getting someone who's not going to stick around. A girl who is attracted to the narcissist who spends that much time manscaping is the kind of girl who you're going to catch banging your fellow bare-chested buddy.

And like me, you'll probably have some hair on your ass. The area where I could have a tramp stamp looks like the Amazon rainforest. I was once paid twenty bucks by your crazy Uncle Ray to shave my ass. I want to make that clear, *he paid me.* He was so disgusted at the briar patch on and around my ass that he coughed up what was probably a half day's pay at the time to see the bramble above my butthole go away.

Ray also paid our friend Dave one hundred dollars to let us shave him. Dave was a hairy motherfucker. He was somewhere between Vic Tayback and Chewbacca. So you can see why Ray would be tempted to see him bald as a baby mouse. He actually threw a Shave Dave party. I was there. Dave stood in Ray's apartment complex driveway, Ray hit him with the hose, then we all sprayed him with shaving cream and took turns with the Bic. It was so much fun that Ray actually started roping people from his apartment building into it. There were a couple of older Asian ladies living below him who had just come back from the market. They were literally carrying grocery bags but Ray managed to charm, or bully, them into taking a turn clearing the brush from Dave's back.

Now, when it comes to pubes, a nice trim is okay. But you don't want to be shaved balls guy. Blades have no business that close to your business. But don't let it overgrow either. You ever see a mailbox with the lawn overgrown around it? It makes the four-by-four post it's sitting on look much shorter. So you get out there with the Weed Whacker and make that post look like the Washington Monument.

The good news is no one wants to see your nuts, anyway. No woman has ever said, "He had such a sexy ball sack." Scrotum is ugly on every man. Brad Pitt's scrotum looks the same as Dick Cheney's. You could set up an experiment where very different famous people put their balls through holes in a piece of plywood and no one would be able to tell whose was whose. This could be a fun reality show, *Celebrity Ball Sack Challenge*. I don't think anyone could correctly match the celebrity . . . unless we threw Lance Armstrong in the mix.

Balls are a pain in the balls. They should retract like landing gear. The sack is just this thing that can get in the way and be injured. Plus, it has more funk per square inch than a decomposing horseshoe crab.

Since I'm on your balls—sorry if that sounded weird—here's a tip. I've found that a light dusting of talc down the boxer briefs will absorb any moisture and smell and give you multiple wearings. Save yourself some electricity and water. That's the kind of environmental tip you won't get from Al Gore. Because he free-balls it.

And on that note, let me suggest you go with boxer briefs. I have come to this conclusion after experiments with both boxers and briefs, and they truly are the best genitalia container.

I never understood boxers. They're cool if you're going down to the lake to swim with the chicks, but not if you're at home alone and your dick is hanging out of the fly. That opening is like a compressed pita or one of those 1960s vagina-looking plastic change purses that you squeeze to open. My ding-a-ling would always pop out of those. So I'd have to do that two finger move where you grab the fabric and do a little butt dip to pop the dick back in. And briefs just ride up on you. I've never been a fan of the tighty-whitey.

But, recently, when I was looking at the pack of boxer briefs I noticed something. I had to bust out the jewelers' loupe to figure out the size. The lettering on the box that tells you the size was literally less than an eighth of an inch. I started thinking about it. They use the same Marky Mark–esque model on the cover of all the underwear packages no matter what size. Size 28 to 32 or 48 to 52 has the same chiseled guy with the six-pack abs on the cover. What gives?

My line of men's underpants will have a package where the model looks like he wears the underwear contained in the box. On the size 44 to 52, there will be a guy who looks like Michael Moore holding a can of Stroh's. This would make it a hell of a lot easier to pick out your size. Instead of squinting, you would just say, "Yep, that's what my fat ass looks like in the mirror." It'd be a job creator, too. That way it won't be the same hairless gay guy for every box. We could kick some of the plus-size long-haul truckers and toll-booth operators some extra work.

A nice bonus would be that my underwear line would moti-vate people to exercise. If you see a guy looking like John Good-man on the box of underwear you're about to purchase, you may decide not to hit the Cinnabon on the way out of the mall and go home and do some crunches instead. It'll be a realistic brand for your belly and butt, I'll call it Gut 'N' Stinc. (Say it fast, and you'll get the joke.)

Feels Like the First Time

Like all young men, you're going to be fully obsessed with losing your virginity. Don't. It's going to be awkward, and it's going to end quickly, so just get it out of the way. But not too soon.

Men are to virginity what women are to pregnancy. It's biologically driven to be incredibly important to us and there's a window that, if you miss it, it'll fuck you up. In either direction. If you get laid too early and too often it becomes a distraction, it feels too good and it becomes your occupation. I had friends who had the ability to play college football, on scholarship. Instead, they just spent their senior years essentially dropped out of school, because they were getting laid and that was a hell of a lot more fun than going to class or practice. But if you wait too long to do the deed, you'll feel like a loser, it will destroy your self-esteem and you'll be chasing it for the rest of your life.

That's why in my will I have set aside a trust for you to spend on a whore if you're still a virgin on your eighteenth birthday.

But be safe. I don't think I need to give another lecture on unwanted kids. So get some condoms. And don't feel awkward about it when you buy them. There's no stigma to that anymore.

When he was a young man, Dr. Drew had a father who was a well-known doctor in his town. Therefore, he knew all the pharmacists. So poor little Drew had to drive to Chinatown to get his condoms without his old man finding out from his underground pharmacist network. Like a junkie, he had to head to the dicey part of town under the cloak of darkness to get his latex fix.

And don't get all up in your head about condom size. The Magnum condom makers know what they're doing. It was brilliant marketing, like the guys who named the Smart Car. "Hey what do you drive?" "I drive a Smart Car." Assholes. The name Magnum is just designed to get guys to buy them. I would like to do a social experiment. I'll open a fake convenience store and put a super-hot blonde chick behind the counter, and watch what happens when guys go in to buy condoms. It will be great to see how many of them buy the Magnums with Kate Upton behind the counter, versus the usual Indian guy.

> Lamb-skin condoms must send a mixed message to guys who like to fuck sheep. And I wonder what the answer would be if you were to talk to a sheep about whether they would rather become a car-seat cover or a condom? If the sheep answers "condom," I think we can assume that sheep is gay. Sure you're sliding into a lady part, but you're going to have some guy coming inside you.

And remember, please, that condoms expire. I think condoms should have a smell like milk, so you can tell when they're no good anymore. Most people are busting out condoms in dimly lit apartments when they're drunk and horny. They'll never know if the thing is expired or broken. But if it stank when you tore open the package you'd know it was time to go visit the Kwik-E-Mart again.

> **MY-DEA**
> I'd like to introduce a line of condoms that feature the image of a birthmark. That way when you cheat on your wife and your mistress identifies you by the very telling birthmark, you can say to your wife, "She's clearly lying, I don't have a birthmark in the shape of Italy on my dick."

Now, I know the condom slows you down a little bit, so be cautious about sex going too long. When you're a teenager, especially after watching a lot of porn, you think that you need to bang away for hours at a time. But after years of listening to Dr. Drew talk to women about their sexual pain, it is pretty clear that they're not as interested in that as you'd think. The whole "he went all night" thing is a myth. Once you're in there count it in dog years. Each minute is seven minutes. Here's a go-to: If you're reaching for the lube and she's reaching for an ice pack, that's a bad sign.

And don't think that you need to get too kinky, either. I know we've all gone *Fifty Shades of Grey* and that there needs to be novelty in the bedroom once in a while, but sex ain't broken. I see a lot of movies, not porno, but regular movies, where food is incorporated into sex. That whole Kim Basinger, Mickey Rourke *9½ Weeks* thing. If you're staring at a twenty-seven-year-old naked Kim Basinger and thinking, "Ehh . . . I'm gonna need some Cool Whip in order to get wood here. I could just take her into the bedroom and have my way with her or I could lay her down on linoleum and cover her in Tabasco and jimmies" that's a problem. I like food and sex, but I don't need to combine them. I like football and sex, I like my dog and sex, I like Coen Brothers' movies and sex, but I try not to combine any of these things. Sex is the one thing that *doesn't* need Cool Whip. I don't need ambrosia salad on my junk. Going to the DMV needs Cool Whip. Not a twenty-seven-year-old nude Kim Basinger.

A Beat About Beating Off

I'll close out this letter with some thoughts on a very important part of life as a man: masturbation. The Jews say you become a man at thirteen. Well, I believe you're a man the first time you find some porn and have at yourself. It's something I call the bate-mitzvah.

I consider myself an expert on this topic. My best days are behind me, but I have so much to teach. Without a guiding hand, literally, you could get the hallowed act all wrong. So let me drop some wisdom about masturbation or, as I call it, jizzdom.

I was a late bloomer. Most boys discover themselves at thirteen. I didn't start beating my meat until I was sixteen. I was at a friend's house. I won't mention him by name to limit the object of humiliation of this story to just me. He asked me if I had ever done that and I ashamedly admitted I hadn't. Like the great mentors of history—John the Baptist to Jesus, Merlin to King Arthur or Mickey to Rocky—he opened me up to a whole new world. He pointed to his electric toothbrush and said, "See that? Fire it up and put it on the back of your weenus." I said, "Huh?" He said, "It feels great. Just go sit on the toilet and do it." (To clarify, it wasn't the brush end. And he had a spare attachment. This wasn't his actual toothbrush.) I did. And thus was simultaneously born my love of masturbation and my hatred of brushing my teeth.

After that first time, I thought, "I'm only good for one or two of these a month." It was a process. Like crème brûlée, it was a once in a while treat. But very quickly, I figured out how to do this efficiently and, dare I say, artfully.

But before I get into the rules of the sacred rite—I call them Spunk Shui—let me express my wild envy of how plentiful porn is today. When I was a teen, there was none. I used to just lay in a field and wait for a cloud to take the shape of a boob. Now there's so much Internet porn guys are spending the majority of the day in their refractory period. The question isn't "Did you beat off today?" it's "*How many times* did you beat off today?" I think all the porn access nowadays is going to make you lose your hunger for the hunt. Your generation isn't even going to bother to date because you can go beg the old lady for a hummer, or you could instead just look at thousands of videos of other chicks giving guys hummers. You'll lose the eye of the tiger. This cannot be. Not for my son.

I was sickened the other day when I was perusing some porn with some busty nineteen-year-old, not a blemish on her, doing unspeakable acts with two dudes (and in high def and *free*). I looked down at the bottom of said video and there were 623 likes and 128 dislikes. Dislikes? How can you dislike that? I want to find the guys who took the time and had the temerity to click "dislike" on the nineteen-year-old Swedish D cup being cornholed. Who are these animals that think, "I don't know, I'm giving this a thumbs down." What, there wasn't enough semen? They didn't get a bowling pin into the mix? When did this become not enough? I want to find these guys and just slap the crap out of them, film it and put it on the Internet and see how many likes it gets.

By the way, in that same session an ad popped up that said, "Tired of masturbating?" I thought, "Nope. Try me again in about one-hundred-fifty years." It was one of those "Hook up with sluts in your neighborhood" ads. I say hit me with that ad when I'm in my refractory period and responding to a bunch of work e-mails. That's when you might get me to try to connect with horny singles in my area. But you caught me at the wrong time. I will have no interest in sex in 10, 9, 8, 7 . . . ahhh.

You kids don't know how easy you have it. Because there was no Internet in my day, the *Sports Illustrated* swimsuit issue used to be jackable.

I know guys who used to beat off to the Adam and Eve or the Frederick's of Hollywood catalogue. Not even porn, but a lingerie catalogue! My lowest point was when I went to a sporting-goods store and fell in love with the model on the raft box. This was a busty chick floating in a pool, holding a lemonade. To me, at age thirteen, not only was she hot, she was a celebrity. I assumed she must have lived in an inflatable mansion somewhere. It would actually make a great documentary to track that chick down. I could probably pull this off now. I have a successful career, she's in her fifties, and it might be fun. But I digress. The point is there is no way the young 'uns of today are fantasizing about raft-box models.

Here is my "I walked three miles in the snow" story to you, Sonny. I watched my first porn at age sixteen. Ray's brother had an 8mm stag film. We had to set up a projector and a screen. If you wanted to beat off back then, your parents couldn't just go out grocery shopping, they had to go to Whole Foods . . . in Spain. They had to go on a cruise for you to have enough time to rub one out.

Ray brought the stag film, literally a black-and-white film, and a projector over to my grandparents', who were in Europe, to set it up. They literally had to be on another continent for us to have enough time to arrange a porn-viewing session. But we couldn't find a white wall to project it on. The best we could find was a white chest of drawers in my grandmother's room, so we showed the movie on that. At one point, I pulled out the middle drawer and said, "Look, 3-D." When the party wrapped up, the film got left behind in my possession, but not the projector. So the next day, I was literally holding the film up to the light and squinting. No jewelers' loupe, just looking at eight millimeters of porn. That's less than a third of an inch, approximately the width of a pencil. Sadly, John Holmes's cock was still bigger than mine.

Yes, watching porn used to be a communal experience. It was so rare that we used to get together, have a party and watch porn. If you had roommates and you were the only guy in the apartment with a DVD player, or, in my day, a VHS player, you had to make sure to hook it up in the living room. Otherwise, your room would become the designated jack zone. It was a philanthropic gesture that not only was good karma, it also kept your roommates' chi off your comforter.

You had to treat your porn like a commodity back in my day. It would get traded and passed around. You would show up at a buddy's house with a shopping bag full of porn magazines and trade them like baseball cards. The aforementioned Dave of the Shave Dave party worked at a convenience store, so he would often pilfer porn (among other things). I'd go to his place and turn it into the floor of the New York Cock Exchange. There'd be heated negotiations. "One *Gent* for two *Milkin' and Poppin's*? Are you nuts?" At one point, it got so tense that Dave's roommate, who worked the third shift, came out and shouted, "Can you keep it down!"

And you'd have to hide your collection. It was a nice treat when you'd put it away for a while and forget about it, only to rediscover it a few months later. That's a pleasure you'll never know. One night, back when porno used to be on VHS tape, after a couple glasses of red wine, I stumbled across my stash and saw one that was named *Head Cleaner*. I got excited until I realized it was an actual head cleaner for a VCR. I still beat off.

And you'll never know the awkwardness of visiting the porn section of the ma-and-pa video store. Now everything streams wirelessly onto all of your devices simultaneously. When I was a teen, there were little local video stores that had the porn section shoehorned into the corner. The entire place was nine hundred square feet, so they took a four-by-four corner and hung Western doors, beads or a shower curtain in the opening. It was like the world's worst—or best—voting booth. If there was anyone else in the store, you'd have to pretend to read the back of the box for *The Treasure of the Sierra Madre* while you waited for them to walk out with their rental before you ducked into the porn section.

One time, I was in that section and an Asian guy came in. It was uncomfortable, because I didn't want to offend him by looking at the Asian section. So I meandered over to the blacks and lesbians. Who knows, I could have been looking at his sister on the box of *Charlie Chan in Her Can*.

And God forbid you had to call in advance to find out if they had the title you wanted. I interviewed the great Ron Jeremy on *Loveline* when he was promoting a movie called *Spank Me, Fuck Me* (featuring number-one Asian big-boob queen, Minka). Given that cast, I had to see it. So the following day I called my local video store. It's the first and last time I ever did that. I used to just wander in and pretend that I've never even heard of porn. "Hmm, what's in this section behind the beaded curtain? Pornography? Okay, I'll try anything once."

So I called and uncomfortably asked for *Spank Me, F' Me*. I didn't even want to say the full *fuck*. The guy didn't know what I was talking about. So I had to ask again, I got really formal. "*Spank Me, F' Me* . . . It's an adult feature." As if that was going to make it better. The guy said "What?" again. After one more round of this I finally said, "*Spank Me, Fuck Me*," and the guy hung up. He must have thought I was making a prank call. But I'd say this, Vivid, you lost yourself a sale with your stupid title.

As weird as it is to think about, porn used to be a marker for where we were in our cultural evolution. Looking at porn titles now shows that we've lost all sense of nuance and subtlety in our society. I was skipping through Pay-per-View and looking at the porn titles recently, and it was all *MILFs Who Crave Black Cranks* and *18 Year Old Anal Loving Asians*. Huh, wonder what those are about? I'm intrigued.

What happened to porn titles where you used to have to use your imagination like *Emmanuel* or *Behind the Green Door*? You knew it was porn, but you didn't know what type. But you and your penis were going to find out.

It's not just porn titles. It's everything. We used to have sandwiches called the Reuben and the Monte Cristo. They used to name sandwiches after celebrities. Now the burgers are "The Double Angus Mushroom Cheddar Bacon Bar-B-Q Thing Between Two Buns That You Put In Your Mouth Sandwich." Everything has to be completely described and on the nose because everyone is a checked-out idiot.

Eventually every porn title is gonna end with ". . . that you masturbate to." In the future, we can look forward to seeing *Barely Legal Lesbians Use a Double-Ended Dildo (and Then You Masturbate to It)*.

Now, let's have a talk about the mess that comes with beating off. I was asked once during a live podcast if I could possibly complain about orgasms. And guess what? I can! If guys were like chicks and could have multiple mess-free orgasms the world would be our oyster. Imagine the VIP room at the strip club if nothing came out of your dick at the end of a spirited lap dance. Actually, we'd probably never leave those strip clubs and society would crash to a halt, but still. Women don't realize how important orgasms are for us. They can't appreciate it. For women, orgasms are like solar energy, they're a renewable resource. For men, they're fossil fuel—there's only so much we can put out. Orgasms are awesome, but a moment later it's like someone hocked a loogie on your belly. You can get hummus out of shag carpet faster than you can get jizz out of thigh hair.

There's no science to where the stuff ends up, either. Once in a blue moon, when you take a piss it goes forked and hits the seat, but it's not like when you take a shit it circles around and hits you in the back of your head. Male ejaculate is just too unpredictable. And it makes double-teaming a chick with a buddy really dangerous. If you get your load on the other guy, your friendship ain't coming back from that. In fact, it will probably lead to a Hatfield and McCoy–style generational dispute. You know what the Bible says: "An eye for an eye, a spooge for a spooge."

Before this gets any creepier than it already is, and before your mother rips her eyes out from the images I'm putting in her head, I'll wrap up with, as promised, my sacred rules for the Art of Spunk Shui.

One of my great accomplishments in life is having this defined by the Urban Dictionary:

> *Spunk Shui: Coined by Adam Carolla: The philosophy of setting up a room or area of the house for masturbation with the intent of not getting inadvertently caught by friends or loved ones.*

I realized this spiritual calling one day when I was at Bill Simmons's house and he was explaining how he was going to set up his guest house/office. He said, "Ace, I'm going to put a wall of TV monitors here and I'll put my computer there." Bill had ignored the first sacred rule of Spunk Shui: never turn your back to the door. I said, "Bill, you're going to tell your wife you've got a column to put to bed but you're really going to be burning the midnight Jergen's because you came down with a bad case of writer's cock. Then the wife will decide to show her support and bring you a cup of tea. The way you have this room currently configured she's looking at your back and the monitors' front, which has the back of some chick in her barely legal debut."

There is both an art and a science to not getting caught beating off. This has happened to me and I don't want it to happen to you, my boy.

When I was eighteen and living in my dad's garage in North Hollywood, I was having a spirited session. Of course, I didn't have any materials at the time. There was no VCR in that garage. There wasn't even a wall. The wall was simply the closed garage door and a little Henry's Roofing Sealer along the bottom. So, as Willy Wonka said, I was entering a world of pure imagination. I was Willy *Wank*-a. In a masterpiece of bad timing, my buddy John decided at that moment to pop in for a visit. And I mean literally pop in. He was an energetic guy and decided he was going to kick open the side door and do a John Belushi "Ha!" entrance. He didn't know at the time what I was doing with my dong; he was just trying to startle me. Well, boy did I have a surprise for him. He, unintentionally, timed it perfectly. I was right at the moment of completion, past the point of no return. His "Ha!" went straight into "Ahhh!" I'm sure it haunts him to this very day. And it definitely traumatized me. I didn't beat off again for a good four hours.

Here are the remaining Seven Sacred Rules of Spunk Shui (as read by Morgan Freeman):

Sacred Rule #2: Location, location, location. It's always wise to place your spankatorium at the end of a long hallway, preferably with a raised foundation and wood flooring. Carpets on slabs can turn a three-hundred-pound mother-in-law in heels into a ninja.

Sacred Rule #3: Lose the lube. This stuff seems like a great idea when you're living at home and your stepmom has a tub of it the size of a ketchup dispenser at Fenway. But wait until you're out on your own and your roommate has cleaned out the last drop of Udder Balm. Any man who experienced the heart and cock-ache of the anyport-in-a-storm, "Fuck it, I'll use Prell" jack knows all too well the slippery slope that is the slippery cock. It's like the alcoholic who can't afford booze and is drinking Sterno. Sonny, I don't want you to "chase the lube dragon." Once you get on that you'll have to go to a rehab or prison to get off of it. It will be calling you like heroin calls a junkie. If I'm already too late, quit now! Just white knuckle it. Pun intended.

Sacred Rule #4: Don't get married to the sound. Either you will have the volume up so loud you won't hear the front door opening or worse, when the old lady's asleep you'll resort to plugging headphones into your computer and you'll end up like Sara Connor's roommate from the first *Terminator*. Whether it's the Blu-ray edition of *Taboo II* or staring at some high-def vids on a 24-inch Mac monitor, if you can't jack in silence it's time to turn in your gui.

Sacred Rule #5: Don't get married to the position. You never know when, or where, your next spank-ortunity will be. Even if you've followed all the other rules of Spunk Shui there are going to be times when you're traveling. It's like teams that play well in domes but suck in cold weather stadiums. You need to be flexible. Literally. And God forbid you have a near death experience. You need to be able to snap one off at thirty-thousand feet in a plane doing a nose-dive or while being chased by a Kodiak bear. You don't want the last thought on your deathbed to be "I wish I had jerked off more." That's bad karma.

Sacred Rule #6: Be into what your wife or girlfriend looks like. This one is more for when you do get caught if you don't adhere to the principles above. Assuming you will eventually get caught, it's best to be watching a chick who looks enough like your wife or girlfriend that she won't be completely offended, but enough like someone new that you can still get wood. I have a friend who's into the MILF thing so it's cool with his forty-year-old wife that he's looking at forty-five-year-old women. But she wouldn't be as cool if he were into busty Latinas in their twenties. So find a site with the same types as your lady, or as I call them, fuck-similes.

Sacred Rule #7: Settle. One way to get caught is to spend too long looking for the perfect thing. You can waste hours upon hours looking at Internet porn. It's like walking down an endless aisle in a virtual porn store the size of Antarctica. But the truth is, you can find something to facilitate the sacred act in a few minutes if you keep your mind as open as your pants.

MY-DEA

I have two inventions to nip this in the bud. The first is an app to connect your laptop, that is, your mobile porn device, to a treadmill or elliptical machine. You'll have to run for the amount of time you want to watch porn. Not while you're actually watching porn. That could lead to a lot of slip-and-fall lawsuits. I mean you have to earn that beat-off time with some exercise. Imagine how fit we'd all be. Well, all men. Though if you're anything like me this would just mean a trip to the Home Depot parking lot to hire some day laborers to hit the treadmill and raise the total time.

My other idea is a little more practical. It's simply a software fix. Single guys should have a lock-out timer for the porn-jack session. You set the time you think you need to complete the task. It then locks you out for four times that period if you go past your limit. If you give yourself thirty minutes and go thirty-one minutes you'll be locked out for two hours. Imagine how productive our society would be with this app. We'd be off for-eign oil, there'd be no cancer and we'd all probably be living on Mars. I've even got a tag line for the ads, "Your cock is on the clock."

I hope that answers all your questions about puberty, Sonny. With the wuss that your grandfather was it's important to me that I teach you about all aspects of becoming a man. It's a confusing and scary process that you're not entirely in control of. Just do your best, and know that you'll be laughing at yourself and how awkward it was for you later in life.

And sorry if it was a little too focused on masturbating, but it's clearly a topic I'm passionate about and upon which I have a lot of wisdom to impart. You're my boy, my heir, and you have some big shoes to fill. I don't want to say I've taken masturbating to the next level but before I started doing it they called it amateur-bating.

☞ iPads and iPods Are Fucking Up How iParent

I CANNOT BEGIN to express the envy that I feel when I see what the entertainment world has to offer my kids in contrast to what I had. Whether it's television, movies, toys or even commercials, what my kids get to enjoy far exceeds the entertainment I got when I was a lad. It's not that we didn't have a television, it's just that growing up my television was deeper than it was wide. It was a thirteen-inch black-and-white Zenith and got three channels. Let me be more specific. It got *all three* channels. That's all we had.

Now my kids have a 70-inch plasma television with so many channels they could watch one a day and not run out for three years. And that's not to mention the Netflix, Hulu, Amazon streaming possibilities.

My kids watch a television that is bigger than they are. If you lay my kids diagonally across the screen, their toes and scalp wouldn't make it to the corners. And if you took the television off the wall and set it on the floor it's bigger than the service porch I called a room growing up.

Yet this ginormous television goes, like all things in their life, wildly unappreciated. They, like all kids now, are completely obsessed with their mobile devices.

I woke up one summer morning last year (I know it was summer because the kids were out of school) and walked by Natalia on the way to make some coffee. She was perched on the sectional sofa in front of Jerry Jones's Jumbotron with whatever *iCarly* or *Dog with a Blog* bullshit Disney Channel was pushing out at the time. But as I passed, I had to do a double take and a double back, because I noticed that she wasn't watching the gigantic show in front of her. She had her nose buried in her iPhone. There was a wall-sized show ten feet from her but she was watching the wallet-sized screen ten inches from her face.

Somehow the kids of today got so spoiled on big that the pendulum swung in the opposite direction and now small is cool. (If only this were true for penises.) I had a tiny television when I was growing up because that was the technology at the time but believe me I would have gladly stepped up to the nineteen inches and basked in the glory of a *Barney Miller* episode. It would have blown my mind to see eight inches of Abe Vigoda.

I think this change is a bad sign for the future. How's it going to pan out? When Natalia's thirteen will she be at an IMAX theater with one eye closed to look at the postage stamp–sized contact lens implant television called iLid?

I'm not joking when I say that Natalia and Sonny are totally obsessed with their mobile devices. One afternoon, we were leaving for some event and I walked into Natalia's room and saw her bedroom window was open. So I told her to shut her screen. She said, "I did." I replied, "I'm looking right at it, and it's wide open. I don't want flies to get in." She then held up her iPad and angrily said, "I did. Look, I shut the screen."

We almost had a very 2014 version of "Who's on First?" going on. No wonder old people are confused by technology. We don't give anything new names. Think about it: window, screen, tweet, bookmark, cookie and spam are all words that used to mean something else. Hell, tablet is simultaneously the oldest and newest means of communication on the planet. We have the same word for the thing Moses carved the Ten Commandments into and what my daughter is Instagramming and selfie-ing from.

If it's not on a tablet and in 3-D and costs at least three hundred fifty dollars, my kids don't give a shit. As I write this, I'm looking out my window at an air hockey table that is being used as a regular table to set junk on because my kids used it once on December 26 and then never again because they're so sucked into the virtual world. Think about the toys and games we old farts had and what our kids would think of them.

Ant Farms: Do you remember ant farms? Ask your parents or grandparents if you don't. (Actually, just Google it. Why have a conversation with those old fucks?) The ant farm was two pieces of plastic half an inch apart with a bunch of dirt in the middle and you'd just stare at it and watch ants dig tunnels. This was the height of entertainment for us. (My generation, not the actual Carollas. That was too costly an item for us. I had to go to my kitchen to look at ants.)

First off, what did you expect the ants to do? They're digging a tunnel. That's what ants do. Big fucking deal. Whose idea was this?

Finally, a reason to bring ants into the house. Don't we spend most of our time trying to keep them out? If you want to see ants, just leave food out on the counter.

But the point is this. If I gave Sonny an ant farm, he'd drug me, put me on my back, take a Lincoln Log, put it in my ass and use the ant farm to hammer it in like he was driving the golden spike.

Venus Fly Trap: We never had one of these at our house, but there was one at the counter of the gardening store up the street. We'd go there just to put our finger in it and watch it slowly close. Could you imagine a kid nowadays being entertained, nay, amazed by this like I was as a youth? No fucking chance.

Shadow Puppets: Yes, back in the day we used to think shadow puppets were entertaining. Someone would hang a sheet, take the shade off the lamp and make something that looked approximately like an ostrich head. That's what we had to fill our sad days. If I attempted to entertain my kids by folding my hands to make a shadow puppet of a bird, they'd flip me the bird.

Fake Rocket or Horse in Front of the Supermarket: When I was a kid, this is what made the trip to the grocery store worthwhile. Not that there were a lot of Carolla family trips to the supermarket. My mom would hit the Full o' Life health food store for some sprouted wheat bread and jicama, while the rest of you readers over thirty-five were riding the fake horsie in front of the Ralph's or Stop & Shop. That thing cost a quarter, and would sort-of vibrate or slowly rock for a minute, yet it was the height of entertainment. If it was the rocket version you held on to a metal disk of a steering wheel that either didn't turn at all or spun in perpetuity.

Every now and again you see these around, but you never see kids on them. They're like the appendix. They used to serve a purpose, but now they're just taking up space. Kids today wouldn't put up with that shit. And more importantly, they'd have no idea how to operate them. I don't think my son or daughter have any idea what a quarter looks like. They'd be trying to swipe Mommy's debit card in the horse's ass.

Vibrating Electric Football Game: This is yet another game I wanted, but never had. This one broke two cardinal rules of the Carolla household—it plugged in and it brought joy. Anything that used electricity, either in the form of household current or batteries, was a no go. More importantly, this went on a tabletop. Anything that required space could never enter our abode. There was no place in my house to set up a game. My room was literally a converted service porch with a water meter still in it, so it wasn't like I could even have friends over and set up a game of Clue on the floor.

This game was basically a vibrator that got flattened. You'd put little plastic football players on and they'd spin in a circle. But it was the opposite of football. Random vibrations would make the guys go in various directions bumping into each other. There was no strategy. If they were playing electric football, Kate Upton would win three out of five against Bill Belichick. The little foam football would invariably get lost and one guy would always fall over and just spin in a circle on the ground like Curly from *The Three Stooges*. Sonny would never have any interest in playing electric football, or as I now call it, *Madden 1973*.

Rock Tumblers: I also wanted a rock tumbler when I was a kid, but we couldn't afford it. So I was told, and this is completely true, to put rocks in a jar, add some water and shake it incessantly. For days, I just held a Mason jar full of rocks and shook it. At some point, the bottom of the glass jar broke free and fell out in a perfect circle without shattering. The rocks still looked exactly the same, but I was able to remove the bottom of that jar like the world's worst jewel thief. That was the end of my rock-tumbling days. Except later, when I used Rock Tumbler as my gay porn name. That's how pathetic I was and how spoiled my kids are. I had to make a DIY version of something they would never take out of the box.

The Viewmaster: Another pathetic toy memory from my childhood. This was the world's worst pair of binoculars. You'd hold them up to your eyes and look at shit you didn't care about. "Here's what the Grand Canyon looks like from the south side." Amazing. If they had photos of Lynda Carter with her top off I'd have been all eyes, but instead you got to see the construction of EPCOT Center. It was a portable version of school slide projector. And as entertaining.

Slinky: This toy is like an accordion that doesn't produce sound and is made of scrap metal. Literally. It's a by-product. It was originally a spring made by a naval engineer to stabilize equipment on ships, but somewhere along the way a genius marketing guy decided it would make for a fun, cheap toy. This is one we could actually afford in my family. And it didn't require batteries or parental involvement. Yet it was still a rip-off. The commercials show it going down stairs, right? Never in the now-seventy-year history of this lame toy has this happened. Definitely not when a young Adam Carolla tried it. Like all things in my home, including my parents, it just sat there.

I think the thing only got popular because of their jingle, though it certainly wouldn't fly today. There'd be a lawsuit by GLAAD. "It's good for a girl or a boy" would become "It is fun for a girl or a boy, or a transgender, or a pansexual or an asexual, gender-neutral human."

The Guinness Book of World Records: I loved this book when I was a kid. I could have never imagined ending up included in the book as the record holder for Most Downloaded Podcast. Portable music players didn't exist until I was a teen and even then a Walkman was way outside of the Carolla budget. We were so pathetic and our self-esteem was so bad my parents had the little known 7-Track player. But anyway, looking back I can't believe that this book was actually entertainment to me and my generation. You'd just stare at a picture the size of a postage stamp and think, "Wow, that crab has really long legs." There weren't even that many pictures. But we all remember the classic ones: the lady with long nails from India, the world's tallest man, the world's longest neck, and the greatest of all being the world's fattest twins on the trail bikes. Sadly, my kids will never know the pleasure of gawking at the world's fattest twins in the *Guinness Book,* for two reasons: They don't read books that aren't in tablet form, and those fat twins are now your average Wal-Mart shoppers.

Boo-ray for Hollywood

My kids, and all modern kids, are spoiled when it comes to the movies. They will never know the pathetic majesty that was the drive-in. These went the way of the dodo when I was in my twenties. The harbinger of doom for these American institutions was when they started having swap meets on the grounds during the daylight hours. Frankly, I'm surprised they hung on as long as they did. It's a crazy business model. You need acres and acres of real estate, tons of concrete, lots of equipment—all for a business that can only operate after sundown. But there was something beautiful about a night at the drive-in. It was always a thrill going from the car to the snack shack, weaving through the cars in the dark, waving at friends. When you're in a movie theater now, going from your seat to the snack bar is a pain in the ass, stepping into someone's spilled soda and pretty much giving the person in the seat next to you a lap dance as you attempt to exit the row. You get in that argument with your wife, "Come on. You go get the Goobers, I got them last time." "Why do I have to do everything?" Yet the drive-in snack shack was about four miles away, but you had no complaints at all about making that trip. Maybe because there was stuff to see, especially people making out in the back of cars.

I think if we're realistic, we can just admit the whole business model was based on backseat boning. Did people not have places to have sex in the '60s and '70s? I guess kids still had the decorum to lie to their parents back then and pretend they weren't having sex. Teenagers had to steal away to the drive-in to finger-blast their best gal while *Rebel Without a Cause* played a hundred yards away, especially if they didn't have a basement. I'm sure when Sonny is sixteen he's just gonna be like, "Hey, Dad, could you clear out? Here's a five. Go down to the liquor store, get yourself a six-pack of Mickey's and drink it in the parking lot. I'll be nailing my girlfriend on your bed."

When I was growing up, our family went to the drive-in once or twice but it was typically a disaster. We were always caught off guard, "Who's got a blanket? The car's parked sideways, Dad. We can't see." But I distinctly remember seeing the cagey veterans of the drive-in, the folks super-committed to this family night out. They had folding chairs, hammocks, quilts and their own popcorn machine. It was like the parking lot at a Jimmy Buffett concert.

Nowadays, taking the kids to a film is a festival of annoyance. I'll start with the aforementioned snack bar.

I'm not one of those guys who complain about the price of movies. Having made two of them, I know how much effort they are to produce and I think the idea of sinking thirteen bucks into something an army of people put a hundred million into isn't that tall an order. But the price of the snacks is a different story. That I can complain about. I'd be fine with the inflated cost of theater popcorn if it were satisfying. But I resent paying thirteen-fifty for a small popcorn. That dollar to calorie ratio is horrible. Weight wise, it's more expensive than cocaine.

More importantly, you never know what you're going to get. Movie popcorn has too much range. It goes from so super salty I can't eat it, to so right that I can't stop myself, to so dry that I'm going to bring it home and use it as blown insulation.

Plus, I don't like when you pay as much for the popcorn as the movie ticket and the girl at the snack counter already has it set aside. I want a fresh scoop of popcorn from the bottom where it's still warm, salty and soaking in coagulated butter. I want to see you digging for gold, baby.

By the way, do yourself a favor and skip the fake butter. Here's how you know the shit is cancerous and horrible for you—it's self-serve. You can top yourself off. If it was real, actual food it would be expensive and they'd dispense it themselves. Plus, anything self-serve is a very ugly American thing. Imagine telling someone in the Third World that all of us have access to unlimited fake butter, as much as we can consume. We could sit under that tap and just squirt it forever like a golden butter bukakke and no one could stop us.

And that fake greasy butter really ruins the movie experience if you're seeing something in 3-D. Every other movie that comes out now is in 3-D, so those silly goggles are ubiquitous. When the kids put them on they smear them with greasy popcorn fingers, so what they're seeing looks like the White Diamonds commercial circa 1987. Everything is in soft focus, like a Barbara Walters interview.

Here's my solution to this smudgy 3-D glasses problem, and it actually involves a solution. Since that artificial butter is completely chemical anyway, why not throw a little glass cleaner in there? That way while your kids are smearing their fingers on the glasses they're actually cleaning them. We'll call it "I Can't Believe It's Not Windex."

And my kids have no idea what a feast the movies are for them. When Lynette takes the kids to the movies they hit the snack counter and walk into the theater with a popcorn, a kosher hot dog, a twenty-ounce soda and an order of curly fries—each. They eat a meal, not a snack. The idea of going to the movies when I was a kid and even slowing down at the snack counter was unimaginable. The Carolla plan was to stop at the liquor store, grab a Three Musketeers and keister it. You had to sneak the snacks.

And with kids and the cost of movies it's not just the tickets and snacks, it's the merchandise. If I go to see a movie with Lynette it costs me fifty dollars by the time we're done with parking, popcorn and drinks. When I take the kids to the movies, not only does it break into triple digits for that night out, the spending doesn't stop even after the credits have. When *Frozen* came out, my bank account got frostbite. I had to buy the soundtrack, ten different Barbie versions of Elsa, a Lego version and thirteen princess outfits for Natalia to dress up in. There was this one-upmanship happening with her friends. Natalia only had the doll and the outfit with the crown, meanwhile her friend Cami had the scale replica of the village and the kid-sized sleigh. So I was considered a worse father than Papa John Phillips because my credit card, and thus Natalia, couldn't keep up. Disney does to my wallet what the Indians do to the buffalo. No part gets wasted. When they're done, there's nothing left.

All I'm saying is this. You parents reading this know raising kids in today's society is hard enough as is without Hollywood and Silicon Valley making it worse. So please, take a stand with me and limit your kids downloading and streaming to my podcasts and independent films only. Thank you.

CHAPTER 11

☞ I'm Not Down with OPP (Over-Praise for Participation)

I'VE LONG SAID that kids today are lazy, fat, self-entitled pussies. And you know what? It is our fault. This chapter is a much-needed smack in the face to all of us, my fellow parents. By softening them up as much as we have, we're setting our kids and our culture up for failure. If we were Japanese, they'd all kill themselves and if we were in a war, we'd all be dead.

Here's how off the rails we've gone in rearing our kids. I noticed one day Sonny was playing with a toy bubble gun. It was like a squirt gun that you load up with the soapy solution and when you pull the trigger, it blows bubbles. Is this how lazy we've gotten? What happened to those little plastic sticks with the hole that you would blow into to make bubbles? Are our kids so pampered that asking them to exhale into a miniature hoop is too tall an order?

Our whole culture is catered to kids and their happiness now. I really noticed this recently when I saw the *Nickelodeon Kids' Choice Awards*. We have a whole awards show dedicated to what kids care about? You know what adults shouldn't care about? What kids care about. I saw a parade of A-list celebrities at this show getting green slime dumped on them and thought, "What have we become?" Seriously, this show gets big stars. Mark Wahlberg, Sandra Bullock, Will Smith and Harrison Ford have all been covered in green slime. Can you imagine Robert Mitchum or Humphrey Bogart doing this? Fuck, no. They'd be on stage in front of an audience full of kids smoking, swirling some Cutty Sark in a rocks glass and telling an unapologetically racist joke about Rhianna.

This appealing to kids at all times has now stepped out of the world entertainment and into politics. Every senator and congressman is on Twitter and has an Instagram account, which is supposed to help them stay in touch with their youth constituency but really just ends up being their downfall when they get caught sending dick pics to an intern. Even President Obama went on Zach Galifianakis's Web series, *Between Two Ferns,* to talk about Obamacare. Nothing against Zach or his show, but I certainly hope the president would prioritize his time better than doing a comedy bit with the guy from *The Hangover.* But Barack had to do that gig. He couldn't expect young people to educate themselves on an issue or to seek out information; he had to show up where they already were to spoon-feed it to them.

So aiming everything at people under eighteen has already ruined movies, music and now politics, but what's killing me is that it's now creeping into the sacred realm of sports. I'm not going to even get into the head-injury issue and how it is going to be the end of Pop

Warner football. I think the "protect the kids" mentality has crept in in an even more insidious way.

A few years ago while everyone in the media was talking about the Richie Incognito bullying story, I thought the bigger and more egregious example of pussifying sports was the Red Sox World Series celebration. When they all went into the locker room to party, David Ortiz, Big Papi, a two-hundred-fifty-pound home-run hitter and the biggest guy on the team, wore a snow-boarding helmet and ski goggles because there was Champagne flying. Can you believe what's going on? We can't even have a Champagne-spray victory celebration without protective gear because someone might get a detached retina.

The novelty of shaking up Champagne and spraying it on a guy goes away if he's wearing a slicker, goggles and a hat. It's no fun spraying your teammate with Champagne if he's dressed like a deck-hand on an Alaskan crab boat.

And the entire locker room was covered in plastic, too. It looked like the front row of a Gallagher concert. You just won the World Series, Red Sox. I'm sure you can hire some folk to clean up the mess the next day. Again, it ruins the fun. This is the equivalent of egging your principal's house while it's tented for fumigation.

And was there an incident to provoke this? Did Carl Yastrzemski die from an errant Champagne cork? Did some Veuve Clicquot in the eye end Steve Garvey's career? Where's the bravery in sports? These guys are supposed to be larger than life heroes we look up to. Bottom line: I want to watch a guy being interviewed while his team-mates do a Champagne golden shower on his hair, not his helmet.

It's not just the wussiness in sports that's killing our kids, they're getting softened up everywhere because our whole culture is over-shadowed by the threat of liability and lawsuits. I was in New York not too long ago doing some gigs and decided to hit the gym in the hotel. There was that big sign on the wall with the usual list of things not to do. Among the "No Smoking" and "No Eating" (as if someone chugging away on an elliptical machine is going to bust out a fondue pot) was "No Horseplay."

Seriously, Marriott, "No Horseplay"? Are you that afraid someone might sue you? I don't think this would hold up in court. I ask you, reader, how many times have you heard a study on the news about this or heard the surgeon general talk about the epidemic of horseplay-related deaths? None. And furthermore, I'd argue that anyone young enough to engage in horseplay wouldn't even know what horseplay is. (For those of you who don't know, horseplay is a disgusting porn genre. The man gets on all fours . . . perhaps I've revealed too much.)

This kind of overly cautious mentality is everywhere today, and it's destroying our kids. Sonny and Natalia came home from school one day in 2012 and I asked them about their day and more specifically what they did at recess. Sonny told me that they had a "walking recess." I had no idea what that was. We certainly didn't have them when I was a kid. He clued me in that a walking recess is one in which there is no running, no balls to kick around and designated "cool zones." It was September, so it was pretty hot, but not scorching. It was in the low eighties. When I was in school, I would have been doing two-a-days and being denied water the entire time. But my kids are sitting in cool zones probably talking about their various nut and legume allergies. Dear schools: Your pussifying my kid with your cool zones is not cool.

We've gone nuts with the sunscreen. When the kids had just turned five there was one night they wanted to go take a dip in the pool. They came up to me at around five forty-five in the evening asking to go swimming. I said sure, and told them to go put on their bathing suits. They quickly came

DADDY, STOP TALKING!

206

down in their swimming gear and as we started to head outside Sonny doubled back, panic stricken. "Daddy, what about sunscreen?" I told him that the sun had gone behind the house and there was no need. There was literally a shadow cast across the pool from the house. Sonny could not deal with this. He insisted he was going to need some sunscreen. I said no, and that it was a waste of time and he should head out to the pool before the sun really went down and it got too cold. They headed outside with Olga while I went upstairs and put my trunks on to do a few cannonballs with them. As I walked out, I heard Sonny ratting me out to the nanny for not slathering his sunblock on. Of course, word of my crime eventually got to Lynette adding to the constantly growing list of grievances and reasons for her to give me the cold shoulder. And thus I got cock-blocked over sunblock.

Then there was the Sunday, correction, the *football* Sunday, I had to spend at the park with the kids in Sonny and Natalia's class, their parents and their teachers for a getting-to-know-you event. When I got there, I walked up behind two dudes of suspect sexuality in yoga pants and shirts with no sleeves and a bunch of five-year-olds in front of them. Yep, yoga in the park for kids. For what? Stress relief? You're five, what's causing you stress? Tough session of Fruit Ninja on the iPad? Zipper broke on your Doc McStuffins backpack? You need to get yourself grounded before that make-or-break finger-painting session? This is what people in Arkansas and Nebraska are thinking of when they make fun of California. When Woody Allen did all those gags about Los Angeles in *Annie Hall,* even he wasn't clever enough to come up with yoga in the park for five-year-olds.

So on top of the cool zones and yoga, our kids are fed a steady diet of unearned praise and self-esteem.

You just need to look at their T-shirts to see how much our kids love themselves. I saw a kid wearing a Nike shirt the other day that read "My Way, All Day." I wanted to take him aside, sit him down and say, "Listen, you little shit. It will be your way all day in 2050 if you don't fuck this part up. Your job right now is to be a kid and listen to adults." It's not even so much what ideas like this are doing to our kids, it's what will happen when these kids become adults. I was driving through Hollywood and saw a guy who looked like a rapper you'd never heard of wearing a hat that read "Fuck Humble." Well, it was a nice society while it lasted.

These snarky T-shirts are all the rage these days, and not just on kids. At one point, Kimmel's brother-in-law decided to start an online T-shirt company. He was one of those guys you'd see constantly rocking that "No Fear" gear, so of course he decided he needed to get into the douchewear game. He very proudly pulled me aside one day to show me his latest T-shirt. It said "Scars Heal, Losing Doesn't." I smiled politely but then had to inform him, "But scars don't heal. *Wounds* heal and leave scars. Scars are the permanent thing that is left behind. Scars never heal. I still have a scar from a vaccination in 1964." There was a prolonged pause of stunned silence before he said, "Shit. I just ordered five thousand of these."

When I was on *Loveline,* a listener once sent me a T-shirt that read "Masturbation Is Not a Crime." I brought it home and did what I do with all the shit people send me (sorry, fans). I put it in a pile to give to the housekeeper. The problem was that my non-English-speaking maid's non-English-speaking husband wore it to work one day and got fired.

This attitude pandemic has really affected Sonny. I was watching basketball with him one night and he told me that even though he's a pretty big Clippers fan, he would *settle* for playing for the Miami Heat. He actually said *settle.* That was his fallback, his safety NBA franchise. There was no doubt he'd be in the league, it was just a matter of going to his favorite or slumming it with the Heat.

This kind of behavior started early with Sonny. Back in his tee-ball days there was one game when he refused to wear his hat. I'm not sure why, but he just didn't want to. I told him to put it on three times before he did it. Lynette then said I had to tell him *why* he needed to put on his hat. What has happened to our society? What happened to the years when you as dad or coach could just yell at a kid to put their hat on and they would? Nowadays, we have to convene a tribunal and bring in a family therapist to make sure it's stated in a supportive, nurturing and positive way. He was on a team that was wearing uniforms. He's supposed to be part of that team and should be doing what they're all doing. But in our current society everybody has to be such an individual there is no such thing as a uniform. And therefore I become a monster for telling him to put one on.

I'm also considered a monster for not hoisting him on my shoulders and celebrating his "home run." It was not a home run. Yes, Sonny scored, but he didn't hit the ball more than forty-two inches from the plate. It was somewhere in between a grounder and a bunt. But the kid who threw to first overshot and the right fielder was picking dandelions, so Sonny was able to round the bases and score. And he even got the game ball with the date written on it. It's on his shelf right now, ironically higher in the air than it ever traveled that day.

I don't think any of this helped Sonny's attitude on the field. When he wasn't able to connect with the ball, did this push him to practice more and try to improve his swing? Nope. He blamed the ball. That's the problem with the artificial self-esteem inflation we're doing. It removes kids' ability to look at their weak spots and fix them. Despite all evidence to the contrary, Sonny still believes, and this is a direct quote, that he could "hit the ball to the moon."

Kids hit the field today, in whatever sport, thinking they know everything there is to know. They don't even want to hear any direction or coaching. Another time, when Sonny was at bat whiffing I was behind the backstop trying to coach him. I shouted to him "Sonny, swing level" at least three times. I wanted him to keep his elbow up. But I realized as I saw him not doing it that he was five and maybe the word "level" wasn't in his vocabulary yet. So I said, "Sonny, do you know what level means?" He looked over his shoulder and very condescendingly shot back, "Yes! We have levels on Angry Birds."

Things really went into overdrive when Sonny was doing track while the 2012 Olympics were all over television. After watching about ten minutes of the Summer Games, he declared that he was going to be a gold-medal sprinter. This is despite the fact that he also declared that his friend Jensen was the fastest second grader on the planet. I guess he thinks he can make up the deficit with pure grit and determination. I had fun sarcastically noting the odds that the two fastest people on the planet sit next to each other in the same school. At least Sonny was realistic enough to know that it wouldn't last forever, and that he would have to fall back on teaching kids how to run.

One day, I spent eight hours broiling at L.A. Valley College for one of Sonny's seemingly never-ending track meets. As soon as he finished his last race, I said to Lynette, "I'll go get the car." I couldn't wait to get the hell out of there and into my cool house with a cold beer. She told me, "No, he has to get his medal." I was confused. He hadn't won the race. He hadn't even placed. He came in eighth. It got extra confusing when I looked and saw that the podium had six spots. Sixth-place level on the podium was as high as a serving tray. The sixth-place runner could have roller-skated up to receive his medal, no problem. Again, Sonny came in eighth, so I wasn't sure how that was considered a podium finish. And he wasn't on the podium; he was in what I would call the drip tray. He stood next to another kid who stood next to the person in sixth place. They might as well have dug a hole to put him in. For his three races, he came in eighth, ninth and another eighth, but he still came home with a Mr. T's neck worth of medallions.

The whole thing got even more insane when they called his name and he snapped into a Usain Bolt victory posture. If Usain Bolt had come in eighth at the Olympics he would have just kept running until he found a cliff to sprint off.

Here's an actual picture of Sonny celebrating another track "victory" a la the 1968 Mexico City Olympics.

This isn't just an L.A. thing either. One of my listeners tweeted to me that at his kids' school they had a track meet and third place was gold, second was platinum and first was double platinum. There literally was no bronze. The ranking system they've had since the inception of the modern Olympics is not good enough for today's princes and princesses, and will certainly destroy their fragile self-esteem.

Don't take all of this the wrong way. I love to see my kids succeed, I just think that as a society we continue to lower the threshold of what is deemed a success in order to not hurt any feelings.

Let me end with this quick note to Sonny for when he reads this later in life.

Son,

I bust balls about the ninth-place finish being a podium finish because I don't want you to settle for that. That game ball on your shelf for your home run is a living reminder of settling for okay instead of great. I used to get participation trophies for my years of playing football. But I have no idea where those are now, because I got rid of them. They meant nothing to me. Those trophies were given to me for simply showing up. They may as well have been handed out on the first day of practice. Instead of that, I want you to feel the pride that comes with doing your best and kicking some ass. Like you did on this day:

This is a picture of you *winning* the 400-meter. That's what I want for you, in all things. And what I want for me. Not in a reflected glory, my-kid-is-great-therefore-I-am-too kind of way. My old man never got his ass off the sofa to go to any of my football games. I could show up and simply settle for attendance, and call that a parenting success compared to him. But I want to cheer you on when you're winning, and push you when you're not pushing yourself. If I've ever gone too far, I'm sorry. It's just that I believe, as a wise man once said, "Scars Heal, Losing Doesn't."

Conclusion: To Sonny and Natalia, on the Definition of Success

AS YOU KNOW by now, I was raised in an environment where success wasn't an option. Yet somehow, I broke the pattern of merely getting by and have a life I enjoy and am proud of. I think this is due, in large part, to surrounding myself with successful people. The ingrained mind-set I had to fight against came into sharp focus when I was with Jimmy Kimmel doing some media. Around season two of *The Man Show*, we sat down for a behind-the-scenes interview for *20/20*. The woman who was interviewing us asked me, "Did you ever have any idea that you'd have this kind of success?" I said, "No. I'm a guy from the Valley who swung hammers and dug ditches. I would've been happy just writing jokes for someone else. I never imagined being in front of the camera, having writers and a staff or a big set." It was true. I would have been happy just being the guy who built the set. She then asked Jimmy the same question about our success. And he said, "I'm surprised it took this long." The interviewer laughed like it was a joke, but Jimmy was dead serious. He was twenty-seven at the time, but he thought he should have been on television at twenty-two. It's a good way to think. When you have that kind of vision, you'll be much more likely to make it happen.

So, Sonny and Natalia, in this final chapter I want to talk to you about success. It was a conversation I never had with my folks, because they never experienced it. I have. And let me tell you something. Success sucks. Never become successful. I'm serious. Avoid being successful at all costs, because once you are, everyone is going to want a piece of you. If you have money, your ne'er-do-well brother-in-law is going to owe you fifty grand, want another sixty and when you tell him, "Not until you pay me back the first fifty" he's going to call you a douchebag and cause a scene at Christmas dinner. Many of the jag-offs that I went to high school or worked construction with back in the day are still hanging around, sucking off my teat. They're decent guys who can't get their shit together and I have too much of a heart to cut them off. Trust me on this. While you may be Planet Success, you're going to be orbited by a bunch of loser moons.

People will come out of the woodwork that you don't even have a connection with. Really. I got a call one day from a guy named Tony Bruno. He's vaguely related to me in some way—he's the brother or son of my dad's cousin. I'm not even sure if it's cousin by blood or "cousin" because he and my dad grew up on the same block in South Philly. Either way, I've never met the guy. He knew I was a showbiz success, and wanted a little help getting his own career started. He was a musician. Long story short, he had a demo he wanted me to get into the right hands. This was in 2010. The reason I'm specific about the year is because the date makes it extra funny, and pathetic, when I tell you that his demo was on cassette.

Be prepared. Once you're successful, chances are that you're going to be called a one-percenter, someone who hangs out on a yacht with Mitt Romney, doesn't pay their fair share of taxes and kills seals. People will assume you had everything handed to you because of white privilege. All of this will make you a target for bullshit lawsuits from people who want to take you down to bring themselves up. As I'm writing this book I'm out six hundred fifty thousand in legal fees, having just fought off patent trolls who sued me and other podcasters for no reason other than to make money off work they did not do. I was a target simply for being successful.

But I know that, like many of my other pieces of advice, you may not heed this one, and either by luck or out of spite become successful. So, kids (and readers), if you want to measure it out and see if you've truly made it or not, go through the checklist below and see where you fall.

❑ *You Have an Enormous Aquarium:* The high-end aquarium is a total rich guy move. The guys who have massive aquariums custom-built into their walls and stuff them full of reef sharks and manta rays they've had flown in from Barbados don't love tropical fish; they love people knowing that they have too much money.

❑ *You Don't Use the Phrase "Right Now" When Describing Your Job:* One way you can tell you're a loser is if when someone asks you what you do for a living you start the sentence with the words "Right now . . ." No true success story ever qualifies it like that. No one has ever said, "Right now I'm an astronaut." It's always, "Right now I'm working at a batting cage, but . . ."

❏ *You Pick the Phone Up on the Second or Third Ring:* If you answer your phone too quickly, it means you're desperate for human contact. You're a sad sack hoping for someone to reach out with good news. If you avoid the phone altogether, you're ducking pissed off relatives, exes and bill collectors. Picking up on the second or third ring means your house is big enough that it takes you a minute to get to the horn, and that you're checking the caller ID to see if it's something you have time to deal with in your busy life.

What do people do when your name pops up on their caller ID? Knowing this is the only insight you need as to where you are in life. We all know that feeling when the phone rings and you see that name and think, "Oh, crap. What does he want? I'll call him back. I'm not up for it right now." Well, are you that person to other people? That should be your first thought every day. Are you the one whose calls get screened? If you are, then you are doing something wrong. No one screens Bill Gates's calls. If everyone thought of that every day, and made the necessary changes to get off everyone's Do Not Call list, we'd have a perfect world.

❏ *You Have No Sunday Night Dread:* If you go to bed every Sunday night with a sinking feeling hoping that your alarm will not only fail to go off, but will grow arms and smother you with a pillow in your sleep, then you've got a shitty life. When you are in a position where heading back to work after a weekend is something you're okay with or maybe even look forward to, you're on the path to success.

❑ *You Have No Exposed Wiring:* In general, how visible the wiring is in your house shows where you are in life. The more wires you see, the worse off you are. Exposed wiring is the worst, like when the coaxial cable is stapled to the wall or just dangling free from the dropped ceiling or, worse yet, climbing through the crack of an opened window because it's being tapped off the unsuspecting neighbor's cable box. Just slightly above that is the square surface wall-mount conduit, the plastic doghouse that covers the wire but still screams loser. Wire buried in the wall is okay, but when you've got some money, you can get an audio/visual guy in there to get you going full wireless; that's the best. The lowest is if you are using a power strip connected to another power strip. That's the *Human Centipede* of electronics.

❑ *You Don't Care What Market Price Is:* Sadly, this little quirk is something I've not been able to work out of my downtrodden DNA. I'm too much of a Carolla to ever order anything that is listed as "Market Price" on a menu. I always assume the market they're speaking of in this context is in a penthouse in Dubai. You know you've arrived when you have a hankering for king crab and just order it, not even curious what the market price is. Slightly related to this is the ultimate power move that my buddy Daniel, a guy who knows how to live the high life, has perfected. This involves the entrée special, one of the things your waiter lists before you order. Daniel will chime in with, "We'll take that, but as an appetizer." No Carolla, even yours truly, has ever uttered those words.

❑ *You Don't Have Grocery Store Club Cards on Your Keychain:* If you decide you need the grocery store savings club card on your keychain at all times so you won't forget to save that eight cents on the store-brand Chex, you're probably not on the Forbes list. There's actually an equation with these things: the more of those cards you have on your keychain, the worse you're doing. I'm not saying that you shouldn't try to save a buck when you can. But please, just stick with the card that goes in your wallet. It's the difference between having a herpes sore on your lip for all to see and the genital herpes hidden safely in your underpants. Nothing will dry up a lady's vagina on a first date like seeing the CVS club card dangling from the keychain when you pick her up.

❑ *You Have a Magnet-Free Kitchen:* It's a good sign if you have no place to stick the kids' drawings and coupons with magnets. That means everything in your kitchen is stainless steel and cost a couple of shekels.

It's gotta be lean years for the magnet manufacturers of America, my second favorite MMA. Back in the day, everything was metal and would grip a magnet. There used to be magnets on every fridge in this country, and I once saw one reading "clean" on one side and "dirty" on the other that you would stick to the dishwasher. Even car dashboards back in the day were metal and could handle a magnetized notepad or compass. But I'm sitting in my kitchen as I write this, and there's not a magnet for miles. Everything in my house is stainless steel or some sort of polymer.

I'm sorry, Sonny, I know this is a bummer. Once when you were around five-and-a-half, you explained to me that you were going to be rich like Daddy and were going to have a big house, too. When I asked you what you were going to do to get rich, you said you were going to sell "super cool magnets." So I hope as you read this that I'm wrong and you are, in fact, a magnet magnate.

❏ *You've Never Taken a Travel Voucher:* We've all heard the announcement before a flight takes off saying it's overbooked, and anyone who is willing to give up their seat and fly the next day will get a voucher good toward their next flight. This happened to me recently when I was taking a trip to San Antonio. And three people got up and sprinted to the counter. I always want to talk to these losers. I don't know if they're doing this because they're super poor or super laid back. What's the thought process behind this move? "Well, Mom's in San Antonio on life support, but I can get a fifty-dollar voucher towards my next flight if I just take a twenty-two-hour nap here at the Cinnabon . . . I'm in."

When they do this on Southwest Airlines, it's even worse because waiting for that flight is a collection of some of the cheapest fucks on the planet as it is. Throw in a voucher, and there's a Black Friday–eqsue stampede to get to that counter. It's a freebie feeding frenzy. It's not like you're going to get a BJ from a Victoria's Secret model, Southwest flyers, you're getting a voucher for Fuddruckers. Settle down.

On this particular day, this was the only flight to San Antonio. So this person giving up their seat would not be able to get there for at least twenty-four hours. I have never had travel plans that flexible. There's a part of me that's jealous, to be honest. I wish I could say, "Eh, I'll go tomorrow. I'll just head home and watch some *Price is Right*." That's how you know these people are losers: They have nowhere to be, and no one waiting for them.

❏ *You Have Places to Sit in Your Bedroom:* Most bedrooms have a bed, a nightstand or two and a dresser. But when you've got furniture in your bedroom dedicated to just sitting, you're in great shape. If there is a reading area with two high-back chairs and a crushed-velvet ottoman, you're doing nicely. If there is a table in the mix, too, that means you're having a lot of food brought to you by the help. You're having breakfast and coffee while reading the *Wall Street Journal.* You've reached an enviable level of success. Having a place to sit in your bedroom means you're doing well, whether it's sipping some tea and reading or watching your wife get banged while filming cuckold porn.

❏ *You've Never Heard More Than One "Good for You" in a Row:* Stick with me on this one. When someone says "good for you" to you more than once, it's a bad sign. One "good for you" is real. The other person is genuinely happy for you. You've achieved some success. The second "good for you" really means "I don't know if I would have done what you did." So that means either that you did something heroic, or you did something stupid and the other person does not want to tell you. But three "good for yous" means you're a pathetic piece of shit. That's the stranger on the bus bench that doesn't want to talk to you anymore and is just trying to get you to shut up. If that person throws in a bonus "there you go" before the "good for you," it says even more. It means that you have turned into the guy rambling to a stranger about your job at the sewage plant. "Good for you. Good for you. There you go. Good for you" means the person you're talking to wishes you'd walk away from them. "There you go" really means "You, go there!"

❏ *You Don't Take Sick Days or Have Back Pain:* The second I started doing what I wanted to do in life, my back pain went away. It wasn't even about the work I used to do, though it was backbreaking. It was more that my old life was soul-breaking. When you're proud of yourself and feeling good, you'll walk tall and won't have back pain.

And when you're truly successful, you won't take any sick days, either. There are a few reasons for this. First, truly successful people are irreplaceable. That's why they get paid well. There's only one Michael Jordan, so he gets paid a shitload, but there are a million people ready to step up and take that job at the rendering plant, so the guy working there gets paid shit. So take away the freedom to be sick, and give yourself a schedule and job where you can't afford to be sick and, magically, you won't. Your body and mind will stay healthy because you're happy.

❏ *You Don't Eat Personal Pizzas:* I've seen a commercial, nay, multiple commercials for the personal pizza. These things have been around for a while, but it just occurred to me recently that the personal pizza is the saddest thing I've ever heard of. Eating pizza should be a communal experience. The guys are coming over to watch the game, you order up a couple of pepperonis and everyone digs in. That's the point of pizza. This is not a food meant to be eaten alone while binge watching *Dr. Who*.

Plus, you can't get a personal pizza right. The ratio is off. Once you get below eight inches there's no way to achieve optimal cheese-to-crust balance. All pizzas should fall between nine inches and fourteen inches. The cheap losers that go for those places where they serve trays of pizza the size of a Winnebago for five bucks know what I'm talking about. That pizza sucks, too.

MY-DEA

I've got a plan to beat the personal pizza problem, too. If you're saying to yourself, "I'm hungry for pizza, but I'm alone" I've created an app that hooks you up with other lonely fat people in your area to eat pizza together. Think Christian Mingle or Tinder, but for pizza. This way you meet other like-minded individuals and you're not crying into your personal pizza. You can post your pictures and interests, people can list their preferred toppings and you get matched up with the right loser to share your pie with. You'll hit reply to the post and say, "Yeah, I'll come by your place . . . well, your folks' place."

❏ *Your Job Doesn't Require a Vest or Apron:* Is there anything sadder than the old guy in the vest who greets you at the Home Depot or Wal-Mart? That seventy-eight-year-old guy who's making minimum wage to hand you the flyer of what's on sale that week?

I want you, Sonny and Natalia, to go meet this guy. I'll grab a couple of milk crates, sit you down in front of him and I'll fire away. "What happened? What went wrong in your life to get you here? Pill addiction? Dropped out of high school? Go ahead, Walt, tell them what happened." This is what I call *Scared Straight—White Edition.*

The close cousin to this guy, except stationed at the exit instead of the entrance, is the receipt checker/security guy. I'll head over to the Home Depot and buy 129 finish washers, thirty-seven joist hangers, fifty-one TICO clips. Inevitably, the receipt will be twenty feet long, and the guy with the GED and the lazy eye will give it a glance and a cursory marking up with a highlighter, then send me on my way. His job is to make you pause for a moment and if you don't start sweating or make a run for it, he'll let you pass. These guys aren't security. They're always overweight, wearing ill-fitting clothes, and missed three out of five of their belt loops. The only weapon they're carrying are way too many keys. This is just the corporation saying to the insurance company, "But we had security posted at the door" when something does go wrong. This guy is the human equivalent of the plastic owl on top of the seafood restaurant. And as intelligent.

All right, kiddies, tally up your score: How did you do? If you fall on the successful side of things, well good for you. Just prepare to get sued.

So, Dad, How Many Jobs Should We Have?

As a guy who has had multiple jobs and multiple careers, please let me pass down a little fatherly advice in this arena. Having multiple gigs is a good thing. There is a certain kind of math that goes into this approach. One job is what most people have and that can either be all you need or not nearly enough. Having three jobs usually means they all pay shit. But when you cross over to a place where you have four jobs, chances are you are a rich person. No one can put in the time to work four minimum-wage jobs to make ends meet. But they might be able to pull off three. So four or more jobs means you're the entrepreneur/businessman/real-estate mogul/celebrity. You're serving on the boards of several companies.

As far as the multiple gigs, to me it's about even numbers. One job, even if it does pay well, can be mind numbing. This is the kind of job where you work at a postal sorting facility from age twenty-one to forty-three and then kill yourself and/or several coworkers. Three is just too much for too little return. Go with two so you have variety and aren't bored, or go with four so that you have so many plates spinning that you've got money trickling in from every direction and you have a cushion of cash in case one of the plates crashes to the floor. That way, you can start another business and start spinning that fourth plate again right away. Now, if you do start a business, make sure it's one that has legs. Create something that people want to buy over and over again. When I was getting my liquor brand, Mangria, off the ground it occurred to me that liquor is a product that people consume and thus need to replenish, often, especially if they are drunks like me. I make much more on booze than I ever will writing books. The person reading this will pass it on to their friends once they're done, or maybe even put it back on the shelf at the Barnes & Noble after flipping through a few pages. The guy who bought Mangria will be pissing it out in a few hours and then buying another bottle. I can sum up my business philosophy with the following phrase: "Don't make toilet seats, make toilet paper."

But take heed: Real entrepreneurs don't call themselves entrepreneurs. I've met several super rich guys, the true one-percenters, at some of my vintage race events and when you ask them what they do they all say "a little of this, a little of that" or "I had a company and I sold it." Those vague answers mean the little of this and little of that is done from a helipad on their yacht. It sounds a little defensive to constantly call yourself an "entrepreneur." That's a little like "right now." It means you haven't had a salary in years. Every time you say "entrepreneur," you lop twenty thousand off your pull for the year. I've met several self-proclaimed entrepreneurs who want advice from me on starting a business, since I've started several. But once I start digging into their schemes, I come to realize they're selling candles or e-cigarettes on Craigslist from their parents' basement.

So I'm not going to tell you to "follow your bliss." Yes, it worked out for Daddy, career-wise. I knew I was funny and have made a living from that. But many people, like everyone who tries out for *American Idol,* for example, are delusional about their skills and talents but got fed so much "You can do anything" and "Don't let anyone hold you back" bullshit by their schools and parents that they will go through life being perpetually disappointed.

When choosing your career path, it's important that you figure out who you are and what you're good at and go in that direction. Try different things. Don't pick one career idea when you're thirteen and devote your life to it. If you put your eggs in that one basket, you'll likely be a failure (unless that career is putting eggs in baskets, in which case, go nuts). Your career will find you, not the other way around. It will be based on the inherent strengths you have. If you're Lebron James, the NBA is a great choice; if you're Danny DeVito, it's not. Maybe it was Danny's "bliss" to play basketball, but guess what? There was no way that was happening.

Factor in all the aspects before you pull the career trigger. Natalia, you once told me that you wanted to be a schoolteacher. I then had to explain to you that teaching is indeed a noble profession, just not one that pays. I remember having a sit-down to say, "You may want to be a schoolteacher when you grow up, but you won't be in a house in the hills like Daddy and driving a loaded Audi like Mama if you do. You'll have a condo in Sherman Oaks and be driving a Jetta."

I'm not poo-pooing an average middle-class job and income. I just think we need to have a little more realism about that life. During career day when the fireman, policeman and nurse are talking about their jobs, we should take the class out to the parking lot to show the kids what those guys drove to the school that day. That way they'll know how little we actually pay those people we routinely refer to as "heroes." If we really walked the walk, they'd be able to roll up to the school in a Jag.

You Kids Have Lost the Meaning of Money

Now I know that, by nature, kids understand the cost of things. Especially you, my children. As I mentioned earlier, you treated the cars in Jay Leno's garage like the rack of candy bars at the grocery-store checkout. Remember, Natalia, when we went to Lowe's to pick out a new light for your room?

We were in that section where they have a hundred and fifty lights dangling from the grid on the ceiling. I asked you to pick out which one you wanted. With no hesitation or thought, just an instant gravitational pull, you pointed to the one that was two hundred and nineteen dollars.

I was blown away. This is Lowe's; I was unaware they even had an option this pricey. I didn't even know they made lights over one-fifty that didn't have fans attached. The lights at Lowe's start at around eighteen bucks and average thirty-nine. They're all stamped out in China. But you found the one that was the shiniest, with all the glitter and spangles. Seven-year-old girls are like largemouth bass. Everything is a lure to them. If it winks at them, they buy it.

I thought I was safe heading to Lowe's. I even threw out the "just get anything you want" line because I'm a baller like that. Of course, you quite literally found the diamond in the rough.

Money has no meaning anymore because every transaction is handled with plastic cards. And soon, we'll just use our phones. You won't even need to swipe a card; you'll scan your iPhone screen. Money used to count for more because you held it in your hands. It's not tangible anymore. My kids have never seen their mom take out cash to pay for anything. I don't even think they'd know what it was. "Mom, why are you handing that person green paper instead of the magical never-ending money card?"

Here's how bad our lack of understanding of money has gotten, and how badly it's affecting our kids. I always look for the little signs that our society is coming apart at the seams. The latest is a public service announcement billboard I saw that read "It Takes Courage to Save Money." I thought that things had taken a turn a few years back when, during the State of the Union, Obama told us it took courage to raise your kids. Now it takes courage to save your own money? Is this what it has come to? We've so lost touch with the value of the almighty dollar that we have to have a public service campaign to remind kids that bread doesn't just appear when you click your heels together?

And what message does this send about keeping your shit together in general? Twenty-five years from now what can my grandkids look forward to as far as PSAs? "It Takes Courage to Sit Up"? "It Takes Courage to Wipe"? "It Takes Courage to Chew and Even More to Swallow"?

I know I'm talking a lot about money, but I want to be clear as we come to a close about one thing. Sure, money helps, but I have a lot of bread and I'm still pissed off all the time. You should make as much money as you can, especially since I won't be leaving you any. But don't expect it to solve all your problems. Trust me, the whole "money doesn't buy happiness" thing is actually true.

When you're poor, you feel that the reason you're unhappy is because you don't have money. "I'm eating at the Shakey's Bunch-of-Lunch buffet again. If I could just afford to go to a nice restaurant I'd be happy." But then, sometimes those people get money and realize their lives are still filled with unhappiness and problems. And now that they can't blame their poverty, they have to start looking within and changing and there's nothing harder or scarier than trying to change your life. If you're unhappy without money, you'll be unhappy with money. Dr. Drew often says that we all hit our mean. Just like we have a biological homeostasis, we have an emotional homeostasis. We're always trying to find balance and get back there when we're out of whack, even if it sucked. So you are who you are, and getting a sixty-inch flat panel television is not going to change that. A little introspection, a little therapy and making different choices might.

I know what I'm talking about. I've been the guy in the Shakey's booth with the Mojo potatoes thinking, "If I could just afford to go to Sizzler, that would be sweet. Then I'd be happy." I could buy a Sizzler franchise right now, and I'm still not happy. And there have been times when I was broke and very happy. When I was a drunk teenager visiting Tijuana and didn't have two pesos to rub together, I was quite happy. Having money doesn't make you happy, *being* happy makes you happy.

And no matter how much money you have, you can't buy friends. If you're rich or poor, it doesn't matter when it comes to friends. You can be broke as shit and still sit around with friends high on pot brownies and watch *Caddyshack* over and over again and laugh your ass off. As I noted earlier, a lot of times money comes between friends and ruins those relationships. You lend an old pal money, never get it back, stop talking to each other and have him be the one pissed at you.

Don't buy into the myth that when you get to the top of the mountain you'll be happy. It's the constant chase that makes the one-percenter the one-percenter. The key to financial and career success is to never be satisfied. But that's not necessarily the key to life success. No matter what you end up doing for a career, have the mind-set that you're never done. Elon Musk, Richard Branson and Oprah wake up hungry every day. Especially Oprah. No one our society has deemed successful ever feels like they're finished. The reason billionaires get mad when they go from the third-richest person on the planet to the eighth is not because they have a couple billion less. That's more money than they, their kids and grandkids and the country of Chile will ever spend. It's because to them, they lost. These are just ultra-competitive guys. They don't see money as a way to purchase things. They see money as units of success. It's simply a measurement of how hard they've worked, how hard they've beaten the competition, how much they've innovated and challenged themselves. But do you think they're always happy?

Here's the real message I want to end with, kids. Even if you don't heed my advice, somehow become rich and successful and manage your money well enough to not fuck up your relationships, even if you can pull off the being rich *and* happy thing . . . what you should really be aiming for is satisfaction and gratitude.

We equate happiness and satisfaction. But they are actually two very different things. Our culture foists this upon us. Our society has created this myth that you'll be satisfied if you can just stop driving that Camry and start driving a Lexus. We watch the Kardashians and *The Real Housewives* and think, "Why don't I have what they have?" We have a constant stream of self-esteem wounds being pumped into our homes and mobile devices. Every commercial, every reality show, is "How come you're not in charge? How come you're not partying on a rooftop? How come you're not walking a red carpet in a designer dress and a million-dollar necklace?" We're taught to be disgruntled at all times, that there's something better out there if we could only afford it.

And then, we're taught not to earn those things. Between the lottery, casinos, subprime mortgages, Wall Street Ponzi schemes and reality shows we're constantly barraged with messages about how everything we want to make our lives better we need to have right *now*. We're either supposed to scratch off a ticket and win our happiness or be so pitiful that Ty Pennington and his bus full of experts come by and fix it for you. But *satisfaction is earned*. Chasing happiness is what drugs, junk food and amusement parks are for. Quick hits. But when you earn it, it's so much sweeter. Going out for a meal is good, but cooking one for yourself feels better. Sucking off a drinking fountain at a high school is not a satisfying experience, but when you've been out running wind sprints it is. It's not the things you accumulate, but how you accumulate them.

When it comes to career, remember success isn't about the job, it's about you. You should have one mode: Work hard and do your best. Put in the same effort every day, no matter where you are on the corporate ladder. Many of my years as a carpenter were spent with me just half-assing it. My tools were disorganized. I wasn't efficient because I knew that I didn't want to be a carpenter for the rest of my life. But what I didn't realize was that the way out of that miserable life was to do what I was doing well. Not to become the foreman, but to just train myself not to be miserable. I needed to flex the mental muscle of giving a shit and putting in effort. I eventually realized that as long as I was stuck doing that work, I was going to do it the best I possibly could. I actually got a lot happier doing the shitty job I didn't want to do by doing it well. And that carried over into other areas of my life.

Don't think about what you're getting paid when you decide how much effort to put into any task. Just put in what it takes. When you have a chore to do and you're putting in a lackluster effort ask yourself this: If it paid ten thousand dollars, would I step up my game? If the answer is yes, then do it. Because putting in the effort is the reward in and of itself.

Whether it's restoring a car, rebuilding a house or writing a book it's all about the process. Let's go with restoring a car first. You look at that thing and think, "It's covered in rust, who knows if we can even salvage it. I really want a shiny red convertible, but I don't want the part where I'm covered in grease and my hands are banged up from rebuilding the engine."

The same comes with remodeling a house. My first house was a disaster. It was a termite-infested death trap. All I could think about was how nice it would be if it had central air and a new kitchen. For people like my mom, that journey would have been devastating. She'd never even start because the task seemed too difficult.

I dreaded writing this book. I've dreaded writing all of my books. It's a long process. The words that are being typed right now will not be read for a year. There will be months of scrutinizing them and rearranging them. It's not a quick, smooth journey.

No matter what the task is, remember, it ain't going to be nonstop fun. It's about *embracing* the journey, not about *enjoying* the journey. No one looks forward to taking a scraper and removing undercoating from the bottom side of a fender, tearing out an old lathe and plaster ceiling or agonizing over the exact right words to best describe how much it sucks writing a book (wait, I just did). But just one person could read this book, and I'd still be satisfied with how it turned out. Would I be happier if it were read by millions? Yes, of course. But my feeling of satisfaction is in the final product and the process of creating it. I mean that.

So with all things, have a goal and have a plan, but throw yourself fully into each step along the way and before you know it, you'll be at your destination. If you can embrace the journey, rather than the outcome, you win.

And gratitude is the key to happiness, plain and simple. Are you happy to be alive? Just being amongst the healthy and living? Your alarm going off, you waking up, getting out of bed and having another day on the planet is enough to be grateful for. A lot of people didn't live to see their twentieth birthdays. A lot of people saw their eightieth, but that was two hundred years ago and they're in the cold ground right now. When you look at the age of the earth and the universe the amount of time we exist and can enjoy life is limited. So soak it all up.

I'm reminded of my dearly departed friend, Philip Wellford, a.k.a. Philip the Juggler. Philip died in December 2012 of early onset dementia. He just fell apart. It was devastating. He was a virile guy. When we were younger, he would be on a unicycle juggling butcher knives. He hiked the John Muir Trail with his father. But in May 2012, I had him onstage with me one last time in Kansas City. He had to wear a helmet and was using a walker. And he was dead seven months later. So if that's not enough of a message about embracing life while you've still got it, I don't know what is.

But just to double down on the gratitude point, here's another Philip story. Around 1999, when *Loveline* was in full bloom and *The Man Show* was taking off, we had a conversation about our careers. He was telling me that he lamented not making it in Hollywood and achieving the success he dreamt of, like a sitcom. He was impressed with where I was in my career and called himself "just a juggler." He had a standing gig opening for Andy Williams in Branson and would do that five nights a week for years. He'd do twenty minutes before Andy came out. This was in a ten-thousand-seat room. Every night. I told him, "Philip, you have not had a job, a real job, for twenty-five years. You don't understand the odds that you beat just being a performer, just having a regular gig. You're not waiting tables right now. You're working. You do twenty minutes a night, then play golf during the day and hang out with your wife in your beautiful home." He was standing on the ninety-ninth step of a pyramid and thinking, "Damn, I didn't make it to the top." So make sure, kids, to look back at those other steps and see how far you've come. Look back at all those people struggling on step one and think, "I'm grateful to be where I'm at."

You've got to grab those moments of gratitude where you can. One afternoon a few years ago, I was driving down Wilshire Boulevard to do an interview at *People* magazine and going straight from there to do a live spot on *The O'Reilly Factor*.

As I was driving, I realized I was about to pass a Pier 1 Imports that I had built many years back during my construction days. One of my worst days, a watershed low point in my construction misery, was building that store. I was working in the lot behind that place and there was a mound of dirt about the size of a Humvee. It was on one end of the parking lot and there was a dumpster on the other. I showed up on a Friday morning at the crack of butt and was handed a shovel and a wheelbarrow and told to go to town. (I remember it was a Friday because at that point, just like Loverboy said, I was working for the weekend.) There was a narrow plank leading up to the doors of the dumpster so I could wheel the barrow into it and dump it out. The foreman told me, "If you hustle, you can get that whole mound moved into the dumpster before you knock off tonight." This was mule work. If it was two hundred years ago and I was black, this would be slave labor.

It felt like something you would do if you were trying to torture someone. It brings to mind two great scenes, from two great movies. It was a hell of a lot like the "What's your dirt doin' in his ditch?" scene from *Cool Hand Luke*. Just mental agony. But it was also like *The Great Escape,* when Steve McQueen's character is in the cooler counting the number of times he can bounce the baseball off the wall just to keep himself sane. I was counting the number of steps between the dirt pile and the dumpster, just to keep my mind from eating itself.

The dumpster was full by five, and I knocked off having made just enough money for a six-pack and the gas that it took me to get to the site.

So even though I was running a few minutes behind already,

I pulled off Wilshire and into the Pier 1. I did a nice victory lap around the parking lot where I had suffered so much misery. It was like MacArthur returning to the Philippines. It felt good. I didn't do donuts or urinate in the lot, just drove the length of it and took a moment to feel some satisfaction, to acknowledge where I had been versus where I was.

Taking time out to feel that gratitude for where you've come to in your journey of life is so crucial. Because of our cultural messages, people treat their lives like there's a party going on and they're not invited. Your life isn't "out there." Maybe it's right under your nose. There's a fantastic John Hiatt song called "You May Already Be A Winner" about a guy who gets a Publisher's Clearing House–type letter in the mail addressed to "Mr. and Mrs. Permanent Dweller" that says, "You May Already Be a Winner." And he realizes that the letter is right.

I know you're tired of the same old dress, I know the car's been repossessed
I know this house is just a shack, but there's this love we can't hold back.

He's satisfied, happy and grateful with what he has. I wish that for you, Sonny and Natalia, and for all of you readers out there and your kids, too. Again, that thing you're chasing is not out there. It's in your garage when you wrench on your car rather than sending it to a mechanic. It's in your yard when you cut your own grass instead of hiring the Mexican to do it. It's in your empty in-box at the end of the week when you've completed your work. It's in your kids' bedroom when you tuck them in for the night.

I've had this moment. It was in October 2011 and I was putting the kids to bed. I was kissing and hugging them after a spirited wrestling match and singing a song that always cracks them up. It's sung to the tune of "Silent Night."

Silent night, holy night
All is calm, all is bright
Round yon HAMBURGER mother and child
Holy HOT DOG so tender and mild

I change up the food every time and it always kills Sonny. He probably laughs harder at this than you have at any line in this book.

It occurred to me that I could have easily not done this. When it came to having kids, I thought, "I'm old enough, I've got a pretty good thing going here. Why mess with it?" And the message I got from my parents was that there was no upside to being a parent. I was a burden to them, why wouldn't my own progeny be a pain in the ass, too? Had I listened to that retarded inner voice, I would have not had you two in my life, Sonny and Natalia. I would be a completely different person with a completely different purpose. I feel a little like a born-again Christian who, once he sees the light, looks back on all the years before like it was someone else living them. If I hadn't gotten past myself and past my shitty upbringing, my life wouldn't be nearly as fulfilling as it is today.

Being a parent is the greatest success. It's the ultimate in long-term thinking. When you're wiping poo-poo and not getting any sleep, you want to kill yourself, but the pride you feel when that kid does something right and shows you that you did your job well, when they have kids of their own and become good parents themselves, that's the payoff. There's no way to look that far down the road, but that's when you feel satisfied. And when you do sense that satisfaction, take a beat and be grateful you could.

So my final piece of fatherly advice, Sonny and Natalia, is to have kids and love them as much as I love you.

Acknowledgments

Thank you to everyone at Dey Street/HarperCollins who told me I should write yet another book that no one in my family will read. This includes Lynn Grady, Sean Newcott, Mandy Kain, Heidi Richter, Shelby Peak and Paula Szafranski.

I should also thank the folks who handle all the business side of the book thing for me—James "Babydoll" Dixon, my agent, Dan Strone, my literary agent, and Dan Bodansky. I'd also like to tip my hat to Mike Lynch, the wizard behind the curtain for all of this.

Finally, to my editor, Carrie Thornton, whose complaints about her own kids brought a greater level of authenticity to my tales of woe.

About the Author

Adam Carolla is the author of the *New York Times* bestsellers *In Fifty Years We'll All Be Chicks, Not Taco Bell Material* and *President Me*, as well as a radio and television host, comedian, and actor. Carolla is well known as the cohost of the syndicated radio and MTV show *Loveline*, as the cocreator and star of *The Man Show* and *Crank Yankers*, and as a contestant on *Dancing with the Stars* and *Celebrity Apprentice*. He currently hosts *Catch a Contractor* and *The Adam Carolla Show*, which is the Guinness World Record holder for Most Downloaded Podcast and is available on iTunes and AdamCarolla.com.